THE YEAR 2020 WAS NOT FOR SISSIES

FAT BOY NEVERMORE

MARÉTHA MARAIS

First Published 2024 by Marétha Marais

Marétha Marais
P.O. Box 1042, Paardekraal, Gauteng, South Africa, 1752
Mobile No +72 82 560 2072
maraismaretha@gmail.com
maretha@vitalitybroadband.co.za

ISBN 978-1-0672377-4-5 (Print)
ISBN 978-1-0672377-3-8 (eBook)

Cover and interior crafted with love by the team at
www.myebook.online

CONTENTS

YEAR 3, MONTH 1, WEEK 1

NEW YEAR'S WISHES

Captain David Zacharias Log

STARDATE 73453.45 LOG ENTRY 212

We'd had the most enormous family Christmas ever. Even Mom's half-brother from Ireland stayed over for Christmas. He only left this morning for parts unknown, as Grandma Edith puts it. The Millers and Sullivans gathered at Grandpa and Grandma Sully's place for Christmas and New Year. Luckily, the farm has lots of bedrooms and cottages, and I only had to share with Liam. I'm certain Grandma Sully will be glad when the family leave after New Year. I'm sure tired of all the people coming and going, listening to the same stories over and over again, always being told to watch the younger kids. But it did take my mind off the looming eighth grade I'd be starting in the new school year.

We Millers do not do New Year resolutions – we do wishes for all the important people in our lives. It's Mom's family that has this tradition, the Sullivans. The rule is that you must write them before twelve on the first day of January. It's already after nine and I better get started, my cousin Liam has finished his and is sitting on the floor busy cleaning his drone-baby. He says he is going to work with drones and drone technology when he leaves school then he can fly drones for his work.

My wish for Mom and Dad is that they will love each other and stay together for ever and ever. My wish for my sister Amelia is that she makes the swim team this year, she's worked really hard at the gym. My wish for all the grandparents is that they stay happy and healthy. For Liam, I wish for him to do well in Grade 12 so that he can go to university. And for Mom's adrenalin junkie brother, Uncle Luke, I wish that he would always be safe when he does that extreme sport stuff.

For my friend Adam, I wish that his auto-immune disease would go away so that he does not have to spend any time in quarantine this year. Although he is over a year younger than me, he is now my bestest friend.

'Are you not done yet? Why are you writing so much this year? You used to be finished first.' Liam gets up from the floor and stretches. He is so much taller now. 'I'm going to shower. Hope there's hot water. Be done when I get back.' He carefully puts the drone on top of the cupboard before he grabs his bathroom stuff.

'Ouch! Why did have to hit me with the towel?'

'To wake you up – finish your wish list, Little Cousin. I'm tired and want to go to sleep. I want to catch the sunrise with my new drone.'

I check my wish list again. I suppose I should make a wish for Khanyi too, but I can't think of anything specific. Since he moved in across the street with his mom and sisters, Remo and Keeya, we have become sort of friends. It was Adam that befriended him. Adam thinks everybody should be friends. I still don't know if I like him much, even if he sometimes talks like Yoda of *Star Wars*.

I hesitate before I write my last wish, because it's a selfish one. I can hear the shower turning off, Liam will be out soon. I take a deep breath and write quickly: I wish that Max and Jennie will always be my friends. When the door opens, I quickly fold up the page and stuff it under my pillow.

'You done? I'm beat. Turn off the light after you've brushed your teeth.'

'I already brushed my teeth. You switch off the light.' It's so dark on the farm that once the light is off you cannot find the bed without bumping into stuff.

'I'm older than you, you should show me some respect. Switch on the torch on your phone and don't switch it off until I tell you to.' Liam takes four big leaps and jumps into bed, and the headboard hits the wall with a thud.

'Liam!' His dad on the other side of the wall shouts at him. It happens every time when it's Liam's turn to switch off the light.

'Are you still afraid that there are monsters under your bed, Older Cousin?' Liam throws a shoe at me and it hits the wall.

'Liam…!'

YEAR 3, MONTH 1, WEEK 2

NOT SO HAPPY NEW YEAR

Captain David Zacharias Log

STARDATE 73483.78 LOG ENTRY 213

Ten days to go to D-day. I wish it were next year already.

It is long past new year, and Grandpa Heinz and Grandma Edith are still in South Africa. You should have seen Grandma's face when she arrived in December and realised, I'd lost more weight and that we were all sticking to our new eating habits. Grandpa Heinz hugged me and said that he was proud of me. Best of all I did not even pick up weight over the holidays, I was always on the move since Liam can't stay still for a minute and I had to help him carry around the stuff for his drones. That stuff is heavy, even in those high-tech carry packs.

We are back home now and the days are counting down to the dreaded new school year. I'll be starting Grade 8 at the same high school as Amelia. But what is tying my stomach into knots is the dreaded three weeks of hazing for all new Grade 8s. We are even called Greenies for the whole of the first term. Amelia says it is orientation and there is no hazing at all, just building team spirit and shaping us into learners Weston High can be proud of. It is easy for her, she's one of the popular girls at school. Me, not so much. With a sigh I cross out yet another day. Ten more days of freedom left.

YEAR 3, MONTH 1, WEEK 3

COUNTING DOWN

Captain David Zacharias Log

Stardate 73503.08 Log Entry 214

1. *We picked up my navy-blue Weston High blazer and tie. Amelia has green and silver piping since she is now in Grade 12. Mine is just green, paired with the white shirt and grey pants from last year.*
2. *No public school for Adam, he's still being home schooled. He has a new teacher for Grade 6 Natural Science and Maths. Miss Emmy will teach the other subjects.*
3. *A very happy Remo is going to Grade R this year at Weston Primary. I hope she is going to make lots of friends.*

I just cannot get away from the new school thing. As soon as I forget about it, someone brings it up again. Just like now when I had to get all dressed up in my new high school uniform so Grandma Edith could take pictures to show the family in Germany. No escape for Amelia either since she is now in Grade 12. Her last year of school before stepping into the adult world, according to Grandma. The pictures took forever, and I was sweating buckets in the hot weather. I couldn't even moan about it as Mom threatened to ground me if I didn't behave and smile properly for the pictures. I was so happy when Grandpa Heinz finally put his foot down and said: *genug ist genug.*

When we go biking and Remo joins us, she talks about nothing else but going to the big school with Khanyi. And that Khanyi is in Grade 7, and he is a prefect. Mom warned me not to tell Remo I don't like school. Khanyi even threatened to hit me if I scare his sister. But I'm so tired of all the school talk. 'Can we please talk about something besides school? It's still the holidays. No-one is allowed to talk about school.'

'Then what do you want to talk about?' I don't like the half-smiley look Khanyi gives me. He's channelling Yoda again, being all wise and adult-like. Remo peeks around his back and sticks out her tongue at me. 'School, school, school…'

And Adam joins in, 'school, school, SCHOOL.'

'Stop it! I'm not playing with you anymore. I'm going home.' I start to pedal faster and at the corner take a left for home.

'Hey, we are going to the park! Davey! Davey, come back.' I pretend not to hear Khanyi. Not even when he tells the other two to stop. 'Hey you two, stop! Davey's right, we should not talk about school during the holidays. Davey, they are sorry, come back.' I don't slow down until they catch up with me and Adam apologises. Remo just hides behind her brother's back and does not talk to me all afternoon, making it very clear that she's angry with me.

YEAR 3, MONTH 1, WEEK 4

COUNTDOWN – 2 DAYS TO GO

Captain David Zacharias Log

STARDATE 73522.41 LOG ENTRY 215

1. *I just know it will be the worst year ever. They can call it what they like, but orientation is just another word for hazing.*
2. *This is going to be a BAD year.*

Step… step… step… I wish I could take off my blazer; it's just stupid to wear a jacket in summer. And the stupid tie is suffocating me. Next to me, Perfect Amelia doesn't care about the heat; she sings along to a song on her earbuds. She notices me watching her and pulls the bud from her ear.

'It is going to be the best year ever! Aren't you happy to start high school?'

'Can you stop smiling? You're not the one going to get harassed for two weeks.'

'You're not going to get harassed – it's orientation. You'll be assigned a student advisor to watch over you. We're civilised at Weston High, not so barbaric like Greenwich and Kallie Joubert.' She gives a delicate shudder before continuing. 'Don't worry –

I'll watch out for you. Cheer up. Remember what Dad always says: with good grace.'

'Yeah, yeah. I know, a positive attitude. It's easy to talk if you are not the one doing it.' I kick a stone out of my way; it hits the streetlight with a solid thunk.

'Where is your Miller backbone today?'

I give her a dirty look.

We turn the corner, and the noise and chaos of the first day hits me in the face. Hooting, kids laughing, calling out to their friends, the whistle of the crosswalk, parents, kids, buses, taxis, and cars everywhere.

'That doesn't look very civilised....'

'Don't worry, little brother; I'll protect you. Carly, Carly over here!' Amelia's best friend since forever pops out from the commotion at the main gate. She is followed by two more of her friends.

'Hi, you're here. Hello, Davey – are you excited to start your high school career? Did you hear that Charl and Kristine broke up over the holidays? She's not even coming back to school. That is a bit extreme, don't you think?'

'Rumour has it that she is pregnant.'

'Dani! That is so untrue! There are kids around. Behave yourself.' Carly holds her hands over my ears.

I pull away. 'It's too late. I already heard it.' I do not want to be part of this conversation, but Carly puts her arm around my shoulder and starts walking us to the gate, still talking.

'She moved to Cape Town, you know. She will stay with her mom now that the divorce is final. Don't spread any rumours. Move people, seniors coming through. Stick with me, and I'll get you safely to the hall.'

Carly is barely taller than me, but the force of her personality parts the blue wave. She never stops talking, greeting friends, giving orders, and conversing with the three riding our tails. At the school gate, I see a flash of white hair like an anime character. There is only one person that I know with super-white hair, and sure enough, a familiar face appears out of the chaos.

'Hey, stop! That's my friend Max.' The train comes to a halt. Max, hands in his pockets, surveys the commotion. When he sees me, he gives a wave and makes his way over to us.

Carly grabs him by the arm. 'Good, now we have two.' The train starts moving again.

'That was so hectic. Who's the girl?' Max sinks down in the seat next to me and stares after the disappearing Carly. 'She never stops talking!'

'Carly? She's my sister's best friend. I thought you were going to Greenwich.'

'Nope – we are halfway between the two, and I liked Weston more. They're better at rugby and sports anyway.'

'And they have dance and drama.'

Max smiles at me. 'That too. Do you think we'll end up in the same class?'

'I hope so. It would be nice.' Seeing Max cheers me up, and for the first time, high school life doesn't look so bleak. If only there were no hazing.

Assembly passes by in a frenzy of both new and familiar rituals. Once done, we are called to line up in our class groups. My guardian angel ensures that Max is in my class, but on the downside – so is Big Henry and snotty Allister, who ate my fist two years ago. The Crunch and Wentworth are in the same class.

First break, the Greenies are ordered to line up. I'm squashed between Max and Mpho, an old rugby teammate from Weston Primary. A familiar twinge makes itself known, and I rub my stomach. The dreaded hazing is about to begin.

'Why are you wearing a tie?'

'Take it off! Greenies do not deserve to wear the school colours. FOLD IT NEATLY – YOU ASS, how can you disrespect the school colours?'

'Put it in your jacket inside pocket – an INSIDE POCKET nitwit. Take off your jackets and hang them up.'

'Did you forget your hanger, Greenie? Every year .... Say thank you to your forward-planning-Sir, who is so kind to provide you with a hanger.'

'Thirty, thirty-one, thirty-two... hold your jackets high. March! We are going to the dungeon.'

'NIT, pick up your school bag. Who said you can litter the school grounds.'

The first group of boys marches off in the direction of the dungeon. Followed not long after by a group of girls. I catch sight of Perfect Amelia, looking neat and beautiful, organising the next group of girls. I recognise the pear-shaped girl, Esha, from Weston. The two of us were used in class to demonstrate different body types; I was the apple because I was really fat and Esha was the pear-shaped body type. But she has lost a lot of weight and is looking more like a small oval now. Teacher said that all body types are beautiful and unique because not even two apples are the same. I had to believe her because Teacher said she is an apple too and she looks nothing like me!

'What are you looking at, Greenie? You are not worthy of looking at the ladies of Weston High. EYES DOWN. Hey, Miller – you got yourself another fan!'

'It seems the new bunch of Greenies has good taste.' I'm glad that Amelia hides the fact that I'm her brother.

'Yes, they do. Converse, huh?'

'Yes, Sir.' I'm wearing one red and one black Chuck Taylor All-Star Converse as per Greenies' dress code.

'Right turn, off to the dungeon you go. LEFT FOOT FIRST.' My steps slow down when I get my first glimpse of the ramp disappearing into a black hole. It really *is* a dungeon. My stomach clenches again. Mpho makes a strange sound behind me.

'Pick up the pace, Greenies. We don't have all day!' I follow the white beacon that is Max's hair down the dark ramp. Our footsteps are eerily silent. Someone giggles nervously. It smells musty, old, and sweaty. We turn the corner. Swinging back and forth slowly, a single flickering bulb casts a dim glow over rows and rows of … lockers.

'Welcome to the dungeon. If anyone so much as breathes a word about the dungeon, you are DEAD! Say it with me – VERY DEAD.'

'VERY DEAD, Sir,' we chorus.

'Take out the picture of your Mommy. Stick it to the top right-hand corner. No other pictures or stickers are allowed. Do you hear me, Greenies?'

'YES, SIR! No other pictures, Sir.'

'What's your name?'

'Big H, Sir.'

The massive twelfth grader looks Henry up and down. 'Big H, you say. Kroll, come here. What does the H stand for? Where's Tiny H?'

'Henry, Sir, and Little H is over there.' He points in the direction of Henry Small, six doors down.

'Damm, Kroll – this Greenie is taller than you.' He turns and writes in black marker Big H on the white nameplate. 'I, Sir Armand the Second, bestow on you the honorary title of Big H. Do your name justice.' He continues down the line. Renaming the Crunch into Crunchy, Small Henry to Little H and Max into Panda since Whitehead is too obvious and Hedwig too cumbersome.

Then Sir Armand stands in front of me. 'Davey, Sir.'

'Davey, you say. I would say Casanova.'

'His nickname is Nuke, Sir. Little Nuke.' Mpho is speaking up.

'Little Nuke. Why?'

'Like the bomb, Sir. Fat Man and Little Boy. He was really fat, and now he isn't.' Big H putting in his two cents. 'He's fast; Sir, plays rugby.' Sir Armand does not look convinced.

'Sir Armand, it pains me, but I must decree that his name is Little Nuke. Have a look.' The head boy holds out his phone. I glimpse a St. Michael's picture before Sir Armand looms over me to write Little Nuke on the locker label.

I'm tired, my stomach hurts, and the day is still not done. Again, the Greenies are lining up, this time to try out for every field and track activity that Weston High can fit into their programme. Currently, we are twisting and turning side to side to warm up under the careful watching eyes of Ross or Rocco, as the seniors call him. When I line up for the hundred metres, Max gives me a ready-for-action smile – his goal is to see if he can beat me on a straight track since he couldn't outrun me while we were playing rugby. I miss the announcement and get away late. Determined not to be the last, I drive my legs, and a few metres down the track, I line up with Max before he pulls away. I finish the race in the bundle with Max finishing half a second earlier.

'Nuke, you started late. You get a do-over; go see Mr Wyngaardt. He is the one with the green armband.'

'Yes, Sir.' I meekly follow Rocco's instruction to find Mr Wyngaardt while Legs and Max set off to try for the hurdles.

YEAR 3, MONTH 1, WEEK 5

GREENIE WEEK TWO

Captain David Zacharias Log

STARDATE 73541.71 LOG ENTRY 216

The result of my first three days at Weston High: Little Nuke is here to stay. I'm signed up to practice 100- and 200-metre sprint, javelin, and shot put at the unholy hour of six in the morning to the delight of Max and Legs.

1. *Only Adam shares in my disgust, mainly because he'll see less of me and is not impressed with anything related to Max.*
2. *Khanyi was his Yoda self and congratulated me on my positive attitude and participation in school events.*

'Aren't you done yet?' Adam is being a pain in the butt. 'I never get to see you. Why are you so slooooow in doing your homework? You used to be quick. Did you stay late at the gym with Max?'

'Hey, there's lots more homework this year. Even you have more homework.' I look at the screen showing Adam's bedroom. 'Did your mom not keep you home because your homework wasn't done? Besides, this stupid athletics is also taking up time. Can't wait for the season to be done.'

'Then rugby will start.' Khanyi, as usual is at my house, lying on my bed reading one of his magazines.

'I'm not going to play rugby. Can we please talk about something else? What time is it? Can we go biking?'

'Too hot, let's go for a swim. Will your mom let us swim?'

'I'll ask.' Off-camera we can hear Adam yelling down the stairs. We can't hear Ms Megan's answer, but Adam's happy yell tells all. Since Mom bought me a sunsuit, I don't mind swimming so much. It looks like a wetsuit, all black with dark blue sleeves and a cool picture of a surfer on the front. Best of all, it hides my white whale stomach. I'm sure Amelia had a hand in it since it's black.

After the swim, we are ready to give the Anaconda a go. That is the name that Adam gave to the BMX obstacle course at the park because in his opinion it looks like a snake that has eaten all kinds of stuff. When we arrive at the park, two men sit in the shade close to the Anaconda. 'Hey, look, it's Father Bosinio!' There is no mistaking the ginormous bulk of Father Bosinio. Adam falls from his bike and grabs the priest around his neck. 'You still here? You did not go back. Are you staying, like forever?'

The Father's booming laugh frightens the birds. 'Hey, my fearless young friends – Adam and Davey. And a new friend.'

'This is Khanyi. He lives across the street from us. He can rap. Look, he made me a pin. That is a turtle, like my nickname. Davey is Nuke, and Khanyi is Yoda because he sometimes talks funny.'

Khanyi cautiously puts out his hand. 'Pleased to meet you, Father.'

I don't care for formality and give the Father a big half hug. He is way too large for my arms to get around. His thick black beard tickles my neck. 'I'm glad you did not go back to Rome. Now you can enjoy the summer and the thunderstorms.'

The skin crinkles around his smiling dark eyes. 'I like your highveld storms. They're mighty, like God. Brings good luck, heh, you met me.'

'Umberto, is that little Adam McKenzie?' We completely forgot about Father Bosinio's white-haired friend. He is trying to get a look at Adam jumping and dancing around the big man. He seems familiar with his pale skin, light blue eyes behind thick lenses, and long thin nose. When he turns to the side, I notice the purplish-red birthmark that looks like two feathery wings covering his left ear and disappearing into his hair. I used to imagine that it was the shadow of the angel on his shoulder. When I asked Father Watson about it, to Mom's embarrassment, he said that it is the most beautiful thing anyone has ever said about his birthmark.

'Father Watson, do you remember me? I'm Davey Miller.' He studies me with his pale blue eyes, then lightly touches his birthmark, a smile creasing his face.

'David Miller, Hank and Bubbles' son. You are all grown up now. I did not even recognise you.' He reaches a shaking hand in my direction. When I touch him, his hand is cold. He pulls me in for a closer look. 'I should have known. It can only be you who sees angels in the ugly things of life, who can be a friend to a boy like Adam.'

'No, Father. It was Adam who said I was his friend. I didn't do anything.' I'm spared from the awkward conversation when Adam pulls me by the hand to ride the Anaconda.

It turned into one of those magical afternoons. We raced the Anaconda, twisting, turning, and jumping the obstacles while Father Bosinio kept time. Our laughter drew in kids from all over the park, and we had team races. The skateboarders also had a go. Father Watson kept a watchful eye while applauding winners and losers alike. We played soccer, ate ice cream, and drank red cooldrink. When Ms Megan came looking for us, she stayed and refereed from the side. Mom and Dad ended their afternoon walk at the park and sat side by side on the grass next to Father Watson, a kid sleeping in his arms while his mother enjoyed the rest.

That was the last time we were all together. On Sunday, Father Kingsley announced that Bishop Watson had passed away in his sleep at the age of 88, two weeks and three days. He left behind no family. Father Kingsley noted that Bishop Watson had a happy passing – he had the biggest smile on his face.

Much later, when I think back to that January afternoon, it makes me sad, and for a long time, I could not look at the pictures of that day.

YEAR 3, MONTH 2, WEEK 6

THE TURTLE VERSUS PANDA

Captain David Zacharias Log

STARDATE 73561.01 LOG ENTRY 217

In-house sports events. It's fun competing against Max, alias the Panda. At least now I don't finish last.

1. *Greenies Concert. Try out for the orchestra – I am not getting onto that stage. Max thinks it will be a hoot. I'm okay with the sports thing but dressing up, singing, and dancing on stage. Not this Miller.*
2. *Find a way to see more of Adam. He is not happy even Khanyi is skipping out on him.*

'Everything is Max. Always Max. I'm supposed to be your best friend, not Max!' Adam is really upset. He is even crying. 'I never get to see you. You said *I* was your best friend!'

I've waited until Thursday morning to tell Adam I would not have time to go biking with him for the second time this week. We have Greenies concert practice right after school until four. My piano lesson has moved to four-thirty, followed by homework. There is no time for biking. Adam does not even try to understand; he logs out, leaving me staring at a blank screen. The whole day went downhill from there.

Sir Rocco yelled at me for slagging off in the 200 metres, and he chased me around the track three times before letting me go. If that was not embarrassing enough, by the time I reached the showers, all the stalls were taken, and I had to use the communal shower. It might have been because everyone was late for class, but no one commented on my white whale stomach. After second break, still worried about Adam not answering my WhatsApp messages, I ended up in the wrong class. Everybody found it hilarious except me, and then I had to explain why I was late to the teacher in the next class. You would have thought I'd finally catch a break, but NO! During practice, my violin's E-string broke, and everybody had to wait while I was restringing – it felt like forever. I cannot wait for this day to be over.

On my way to my piano lesson, I call Adam. No answer – he's still ignoring me. He's as good with the silent treatment as Amelia. I hope it is not going to be like our last fight. It took a thunderstorm and a priest to put our friendship back on track. Adam's tears are haunting me.

'Davey, for goodness' sake! Where is your head today? Try that piece again. Start from the beginning and this time concentrate. If you play like this in the exam, you shall fail.'

I look up at Ms Roux. She is glaring at me over gold-rimmed glasses. 'Sorry, Ma'am. I was just wondering if I could take up the violin again. Would it be possible to bring a friend that plays the guitar, and then you can teach us together?'

'That would be an interesting combination. You are talking about Adam?'

'Yes, Ma'am. He has taught himself to play the guitar and is getting very good at it. I thought we could play music together and see more of each other. I'm so busy with homework and everything else.' I put on my best sad face and make my voice sound all lost and unhappy. 'Please, Ma'am, will you just think about it.'

Ms Roux pulls the pencil from her lavender grey hair and chews at the back. Then she starts tapping the piano with a pencil. 'You play while I think.'

I take a deep breath and concentrate on playing the piece without a single mistake. When the last note sounds, I put my hands on my lap and await Ms Roux's verdict. She sits down and starts chewing on the pencil again. I can smell her floral perfume mixed with the minty gum she is chewing. 'Very good. That is how you should play it in the exam. What do your parents say about changing back to the violin?'

'I thought I'd ask you first, Ma'am. I don't think it would be a problem since I'm still playing music.' That is the only rule Mom holds over us. We must all play a musical instrument. Perfect Amelia started on piano and now plays an electronic keyboard. Dad plays the trumpet, Mom the piano, and sometimes the flute and I mostly play the violin. Uncle Sean usually sits me down before a set to brush up on my fiddle technique, as he calls it. Uncle Sean is fantastic. I sometimes stop to watch him play his dark blue viola – his fingers dancing on the strings, the bow dipping and sliding, his foot tapping out the time. When he fiddles, you want to dance.

'Why did you stop with the violin? You enjoyed it and scored higher in the violin exam than on the piano.' Ms Roux is watching me over her specs. The pencil is now twirling around her fingers.

'The kids were teasing me, so I stopped.'

For a long time, Ms Roux only stares at me. Then she shakes her head. 'Damm, kids can be so cruel sometimes. Won't the teasing start again when you take the violin to school?'

'I can ask Adam to bring it when we have a lesson. Please, Ma'am – he would really like it if we could do something together. He has felt left out since I started high school, gym, sport, rugby, Max… and everything.' I put on my best puppy-dog face.

The pencil slips from Ms Roux's fingers and clatters onto the wood floor. 'Davey?' She takes off her glasses and vigorously polishes them with the edge of her dark purple blouse. She squints at them and then puts them back. 'Sport, you say. Like rugby?'

'Yes, Ma'am.'

'Why?' Her voice is a bit high and squeaky, puzzled by this very un-Davey-like activity.

'Because of Khanyi and Max, Ma'am.' Ma'am makes a rolling motion with her hand; she needs more information. 'Khanyi said I had to play rugby to earn respect. Max said it would be fun to try out for athletics since he cannot outrun me when we play rugby. He wants to see if he can catch me if we run a hundred metres straight.'

'Respect?' Still the squeaky voice. 'How?'

'I haven't figured that out yet, Ma'am. Khanyi sometimes talks like Yoda.'

'Who's Yoda?' Ms Roux stares at me like I'm a stranger who has wandered into her music class – not the same fat old Davey who has been taking music lessons for the past eight years.

'He is a character in *Star Wars*. He is very wise and talks funny. Khanyi talks funny like him.'

Ms Roux picks up the pencil. She puts it on the side of the piano; it rolls off again. We both stare at the yellow pencil on the shiny brown wood floor. After a few silent seconds, Ms Roux fists her greying hair. 'Davey…' She takes a deep breath and starts again. 'Davey, dear, it's okay if you do not want to do everything your friends want you to do. It can be challenging to say no, sometimes – you know. Did you talk to your parents about these Khanyi and Max persons? The way they are bullying you.' I'm surprised that Ms Roux is so upset. Her fluttering hands, for once, clasped tightly together.

'It's okay, Ma'am. I decided to play rugby since it was my last year in primary school and I wanted something to show for it.' I touch her arm. 'And the track and field items are not so bad. I'm somewhat good at it. I don't come last in the races.'

'Only if you are sure, Davey. I can talk to your parents, you know.'

I smile at her. 'It is okay, Ms Roux. Everything worked out fine. We are sort of friends now, but they won't be taking music lessons with us.' That makes her smile.

'Okay. Back to music again.' She seems relieved to get back to the familiar routine.

YEAR 3, MONTH 2, WEEK 7

THE NUKE, THE GIRL AND A MOUSE

Captain David Zacharias Log

STARDATE 73580.31 LOG ENTRY 218

In-house sports event – happy to report that I came second in the 100 metres. The first two go to the Inter-school meet. Davey Miller will represent Weston High in the 100m, javelin, and shot put. Crunchy crunched the school record in the shot put. Amelia is competing in the 400m hurdles and relay.

1. *Greenies concert –playing the violin in the orchestra. By the end of this week, no more concert practice. Can't wait.*
2. *Mom agreed to me changing to the violin, but only after the exam and if Ms Megan says it is okay for Adam to take guitar lessons. The moody Ms Megan disappeared since the start of Feb and I am sure she'll say yes since she is much nicer now.*

After concert practice Max grabs me by the arm. 'Come meet my brother. He is a genius but has no social skills whatsoever. You'll like him when you get to know him.' Max keeps pulling me in the direction of a familiar-looking, white-haired boy. I have no choice but to follow. 'Hi, Mikhail, when did you arrive?'

'At 15:28.'

'Walked right into that one, didn't I? Are you with the parents?'

'No.'

'Davey, meet my brother Mikhail. This is my friend Davey.'

Mikhail nods in my direction. His piercing light blue eyes give me a quick scan. He nods, turns, and starts walking with long, easy strides. I look at Max. 'Do not mind him – like I said, no social skills. We run to catch up. 'Are you going to stay for a while?'

From their strange conversation, I learn he is a student at Oxford University in London. Their parents are in New York. Mikhail is not happy that Uncle Gregory is still in the house; he shall tell him to leave. Babi, who seems to be their granny, is coming down to stay with Maximilian. Max is happy about that, but staying with their housekeeper Miss May is okay. I leave them at the corner of West and Poppy. Mikhail does not say goodbye, just the strange head nod again.

I had just finished most of my Maths homework when Adam rang the bell. We had made up over the weekend. I promised we'd go biking no matter how busy my day was, even if it was just around the block. I'm glad we are back to our old routine. 'Is that a new tee?' Adam looks smart in a dark blue T-shirt with a 3D astronaut flying in space above the earth.

'Yes, Mommy bought it for me. She promised that if I scored 90% in Math and Science, I could pick out a T-shirt from the online store.'

'Yo, are we biking or chatting? I have homework.' Grumpy Yoda has shown up. 'Nice fit – told you Lightinthebox has cool stuff. If only…' He rolls his eyes in my direction.

'Hey, don't start on me! Race you to the Sky House!' I take

off, and the other two chase after me, to the modern glass cube house down the road. When the sun is going down it looks like the house is floating as only first floor is lit up. Khanyi only manages to catch me on the last block. It seems the gym and sports practice are paying off. I'm no longer the last one in.

When I get home dinner is ready. We must rush since the first of the four-day concerts starts tonight. Mom and Dad will attend on Friday. I dig into the grilled spicy chicken and pineapple. I like how charred pineapple tastes sweeter. The quinoa has a bite – Mom has started experimenting with jalapenos and capers. She kept the heat down this time, and I did not need the yoghurt to douse the fire.

'Are you nervous about tonight?' Amelia is drumming her fingers on the table.

'I won't embarrass you, you know.'

She puts her hand on her lap. 'No, not worried. I … I don't want to be late. You did check your strings?'

'Yes, and extra strings. I'm the one performing. You should tell me to stop worrying.'

'I'm not worried. I want everything to be perfect.' She pulls on her blond braid, her worrying sign. Even in her school uniform, she looks fantastic. 'Weston won the Greenies concert trophy two years in a row – we are not going to lose it in my year. Rutan High has created a musical with two very talented solo singers. Even their dance numbers are so professional. It is all over the web.'

'A musical is not a concert, is it? And how do you include over a hundred Greenies in a musical? You said all of us must take the stage. More importantly, you had better not tell Max he is not professional. We are lucky to have him. He was accepted by the Arts and Music School, where Khanyi's mother is the principal.'

'That's not what I mean.'

'Then what did you mean? That we are not to Miss Perfect's standard of perfection?'

'That is enough, you two. You do the hard work, and the results will speak for themselves.' Dad gives both of us a stern look. No fighting at the dinner table is one of the Miller rules. I wisely lower my eyes and take a bite of the quinoa, savouring the spicing flavour.

Since tonight is the dress rehearsal and there are fewer people, Ms Megan agreed to let Adam attend the concert. She is driving us today with a subdued Adam riding shotgun. He must have gotten a talking-to, but it was not enough to stop the questions.

'Will I be able to see you play the violin on stage? Are Big H and his rugby team also in the concert? 'Is Max going to be there?'

'Yes, yes and yes. Max is dancing and playing the guitar.'

'I can play the guitar too. Dancing is just stupid.'

'Adam, we talked about this – remember?' Ms Megan makes big eyes at Adam, and he puts his finger to his lips. Yip, she must have given him the be-nice-or-else speech.

'I've bought you a programme. It has everybody's name in it.' He eagerly scans the programme and points out all the names he knows.

Our concert title is *All Around the World*. Even the orchestra gets stage time. My first on-stage number is an Irish jig with a green hat and suspenders. Three of the Greenies can do Irish folk dancing. They tried to hide it, but social media is horrible at keeping secrets. Even if Max had tried to hide his ballet, the seniors would have called him out the same way they did our Spanish guitarist of the evening. I like the fast Spanish music and lively castanets and I don't mind accompanying the Spanish dancers with him on stage. However, this is not even the best hidden talent that was uncovered. Wentworth turns out to be an excellent percussionist. He and his fellow drummers rock the hall in a drum battle. Big H can play the concertina, but the best secret of all was Crunchy.

Near the end of the first day of concert practice, we all had to test for the choir, and that was when Sir Armand caught Crunchy mouthing the words, not singing. He told Crunchy to sing, but he stubbornly just kept mumbling. No matter what the seniors threatened, Crunchy did not sing. Then, a tiny woman with wild brown hair – a mini-Crunchy by the hand – entered the hall, probably wondering why we were late in finishing up practice. Crunchy's mom only had to say his name sternly, and the Crunch started to sing. Think Barry White meeting Tim Foust of Home Free in the "Misty Mountain" soundtrack. The Weston High anthem has never sounded so good – he floored us all. I can't wait for his duet with Tumi.

Wednesday dress rehearsal – all good, no problems.
Thursday evening – no problems
Friday… on Friday, the Miller curse strikes.

Friday's Greenie concert starts as usual. No problems navigating the dimly lit stairs from the orchestra pit to the stage for the Irish part of the show. Score one for Davey Miller. I finish the Irish jig with a flourish that would make Uncle Sean proud. Since it is my turn to play the violin for the jazz set in New York, I give my violin to the stagehand to take across while I get rid of the leprechaun costume – off comes the green top hat, suspenders and bow tie. I grab the black waistcoat and hat. Stick the hat on my head and walk across the blue-painted sea to New York. That is when disaster strikes… As I pass Sabine, a tiny brown blur flashes past us. A high-pitched screech fills the air, and she jumps on my back. She is choking the life out of me while screaming in my ear. My arm is stuck half in, half out of my jacket sleeve. I can't get it out, and the banshee on my back is wailing, clinging on tightly. Her legs are crushing my lungs. Desperation gives me strength; a tearing sound and my arm is free – I pull at the tentacles around my throat. As soon as I get rid of one arm, the other is back. No matter what I do, she hangs on, screaming at the top of her lungs. Black spots start to dance in front of my eyes. I stumble, fall over a chair, and crash into the piano. Finally, she lets go and scrambles onto the piano, sirens still going. Sir Rocco to the rescue. He scoops her off the piano and exits stage right, all the while talking to her to calm her down.

'Hey, Nuke, what were you the most afraid of – Sabine or the mouse?' Never have I ever hated Wentworth so much.

YEAR 3, MONTH 2, WEEK 8

SECRETS

Captain David Zacharias Log

STARDATE 73599.61 LOG ENTRY 219

Yeah, all over the web. Only Mom cared about me being choked to death. I was hoarse for nearly three days and had scratches all over my neck. Adam keeps acting out me stumbling around and falling over the chair. It does look funny. Khanyi took one look at me and burst out laughing. He is not my friend. Max at least tries not to laugh in my face. Miss Perfect is only grateful that the judges attended the Saturday show, not the Friday fiasco. As if it was my fault.

1. *Now I must deal with this concert mess at the inter-school meet. I wish I didn't have to go. When I mentioned it at dinner, Dad told me that adversity builds character. No sympathy at all.*

Walking home on Thursday, a familiar sound makes me stop and turn around. Jennie. She brings her bike to a halt.

'Found you. Hi.' Jennie gives a small wave.

'Hello.' She looks pretty with her pink helmet and big caramel eyes. 'Why are you looking for me?'

'To see if you are all right.'

I can feel the red tide creeping up my face. 'Yeah, I'm okay.'

'You still sound a bit hoarse. She was strangling you.' She pulls her helmet off and hooks it over the handles of her bike.

'H...how did you know? I mean, about practice?'

'Sunny told me. Where are you going? This is not the way home. Can I walk with you?'

'Piano class. Yes, if you want to.' We start walking again. So Sunny is keeping an eye on me as she promised. The year before last, I was angry all the time and I made Jennie cry when she was nice to me. Her sister Sunny, who is in the same class as Amelia, said she will cut me from gullet to gut if I ever make Jennie cry again. She scared the daylights out of me as she was carrying her two swords from martial arts practice with her and she was forever following me and even told Jennie not to be my friend. A quick check, but I cannot see Sunny and her tiger swords lurking behind a tree.

'Why piano class when you play the violin?'

'Long story, but starting next month, I'll be playing the violin again. Do you play?'

'Yes, piano and a traditional Chinese flute called a dizi.' She holds up her phone with a picture of her playing the flute, standing next to Sunny, holding another strange instrument that looks like a guitar. 'This is called a pipa.' Her grandpa also insists that everyone in the family plays a musical instrument to ensure the musical traditions of the old country are preserved. She shows me her aunt, playing a strange rectangular box with seven strings; Jennie calls it a *guqin.* Her aunt is beautiful with black hair and white skin, but the young girl standing next to her catches my eye. She is tall, not really smiling, looking directly at the camera with dark, serious eyes. Her long black hair falls well below her waist. She is wearing a traditional red dress with gold and pink embroidered flowers. 'Is that Sunny?'

Jenny giggles. 'Yes, but not so scary now.' I cannot prevent the red tide from colouring my face.

'This is me.' I stop in front of the lavender gate. 'Will you be okay getting back?'

'Yes, Sunny is still at school. I'll meet up with her. See you next week, same time?' She rings the bell and disappears around the corner.

The inter-school meet on Friday went okay. Only one kid pretended to be strangled while stumbling around. The most irritating part was the giggling girls looking away when I looked at them. I came third in the 100 metres and the shot put and second in the javelin. Crunchy set another shot put record, but nobody dared to say anything about his singing voice. Legs and Max came in second and third in the 200 hurdles. Max won the 200 metres. Legs also won the under-14 high jump. Amelia came in first in the 400 metres, but Weston lost the meet to Rutan High. I hope it is not a premonition of things to come. The Greenies concert trophy will only be awarded at the end of the month.

Saturday morning, my phone wakes me. Bleary-eyed, I grab the offending piece of equipment. I try to see who's calling, but my eyes do not want to open. 'Who's this?'

'Aren't you up yet? Don't you play the piano exam today? Did you practice yesterday? Are you going to practice at Ms Roux today? Can I come with you?'

'ADAM! What time is it?'

'Just after seven. Why are you not up yet?'

'Because it is Saturday, and my exam is only at eleven today. I'm sleeping in.' I regret my big mouth telling Adam about taking guitar lessons after finishing my exam; he has been hounding me ever since.

'The sun is already up. What time are you going to practice? Can I come with you?'

'No. Call me after eight.'

'But you are already awake. Do you want to hear me play?'

I press the red button and pull the blankets over my head.

Adam called at the same time my eight o'clock alarm went off. I should have kept my mouth shut.

YEAR 3, MONTH 2, WEEK 9

AN UNEXPECTED TURN OF EVENTS

Captain David Zacharias Log

STARDATE 73618.90 LOG ENTRY 220

Miss Perfect is acting all weird.

1. *I hope that Adam will calm down after our music lesson. His enthusiasm is too much for me to take.*
2. *It will be nice to see Jennie again.*

'Davey, hurry up – we are going to be late.' This is the second morning in a row that Amelia has walked to school with me. After the first week, she only walked with us on Tuesdays and Fridays, but she's been waiting for me every day, even after school, for the past week and a half.

'I'm coming!' I grab my jacket, a tie and rush downstairs. 'Bye, Mom!'

'Did you take your lunch?' I stop short; I can't go to school without the yummy lunch Mom packed this morning. She made freshly baked sweet potato muffins with cinnamon, ala Jamie Oliver. She also added some oat cookies and finely sliced red and green apples. But what I'm looking forward to is the Marmite popcorn. Now that caramel popcorn is off the list, my new favourite is popcorn coated in salty Marmite butter.

'Wait, I have your lunch. Can we go now? Why don't you pack your bag in the evenings?'

'I did pack my bag – I was talking to Adam. Why are you walking to school with us? Hi Khanyi, did you finish your art project? Can I see it?' Khanyi had to do a comic strip depicting an Afrikaans idiom for art class. 'Which one did you decide to use?'

'The one about hanging on a branch. Have a look.' Khanyi has drawn a man on a roof, slipping and falling, catching a branch on his way down. A guy runs toward the tree with a ladder but puts the ladder down to answer the phone. 'It means to hang on a second.'

'I like it. Look at his eyes popping out. It's funny.'

'You draw very well. Are you joining your sister at the Arts and Music School next year?' Amelia is also looking at the comic strip.

'I dunno. It is still a long time off.'

'Not really, seven…eight months from now. And before you know it, the year will be done.' What is it with her? She's acting weird and always talking about time.

We reach Weston Primary's gate, and Khanyi stuffs the strip in his bag. 'Hey, when are we starting the games in the park again? Do you think we can still play now that you are in high school? You are still going to play rugby?'

'I'll ask Big H today.' I watch Khanyi disappear into the blue wave.

'Are you going to play rugby again?'

'What? I don't know. Why are you walking to school? You used to catch a lift with Carly.'

'I want to walk to school with you. It's the last year we are in school together.' There she goes again, talking as if our time is up. 'I missed out on all your adventures last year.' She links her arm through mine as if it is something we do every day.

'What are you doing? Let go of me!' She gives me a big smile. 'Hey, I don't want people to know you are my sister. They'll think I'm adopted or something.'

'Too late – they already figured out that the Nuke is my brother.' I dodge her arm.

Okay, okay, I'll walk with you, but no touching. Stay over on your side.' She bumps my shoulder before putting some much-needed space between us. We walk a block in silence.

'Are you sad that you did not make it onto the swim team?' At the beginning of the school term, Amelia tried out but only managed to make it as a reserve. It seems the gym training did help but not enough. Swim reserves rarely get to swim in meets. She is quiet after I ask the question; I didn't think she would answer me, but she does.

'I'm not sad. A bit disappointed, perhaps.' She falls silent again. 'But it is good. Now we can go to sports events together. I'm glad you are on the javelin team. Don't you dare lose – I want us to compete for the West Rand and then Gauteng. Two Millers on the same team one last time.'

'What is it with you and time? Are you going somewhere?' I don't get to hear the answer. The force of nature, also known as Carly, greets us when we reach the school gate.

'You won't believe this! Little Miller, get going; this is not for your ears.' She waves me away. I gladly take the opportunity to escape.

So much for the news being a secret. By the first break, it was all over the school: Rutan High had been disqualified from the competition.

'I told you! I told you that a professional choreographed those dances. I can spot the difference immediately. Give me a high five. If you are good – you are good.' Max does a happy dance and tells anyone and everyone that he saw it coming. Rutan's disqualification does not mean we are a shoo-in for the win. Kallie Joubert's Rock Revue has also scored a lot of likes on social media. We still have to wait until the end of the week to know the results. I wonder if Amelia is now less worried.

Waiting for Thursday and knowing I would see Jennie again makes me nervous. I even convinced myself that she would not show up. But I still add an extra water bottle with strawberries and cucumber slices to my school bag. I remember from last year that she liked it the most. When I turn the corner, she is already waiting for me. Today her hair is in a high ponytail; she's chewing the ends while waiting.

'I thought I missed you.'

I shake my head. 'No, not likely. Adam will never talk to me again if I cancel our music lesson. There would have to be a world disaster if I wanted to miss a lesson. Even then, he would find a way to make it happen.' That makes her laugh.

'Are you and Adam starting a band?'

'Oh no. Nothing like that. Here, I remember you like strawberries. You can return the bottle next time.' While we walk, I tell her about Adam feeling left out and the idea for the music lessons.

'Adam is so lucky to have you as his friend.' She's looking at me rather intently. I'm embarrassed by the praise and the strange look on her face.

'It's not like that – Adam said I was his friend first. And… and he never gave up on me even when we were fighting. He's a good friend. My best friend.'

'You are so sweet. And you don't even know it.' Then she kisses me. On the cheek. When I return to earth, she has already turned the corner, the bell ringing its goodbye. I find myself in front of the lavender gate. Adam and Ms Megan are chatting on the stoep with Ms Roux.

I do not remember a single thing about our first music lesson. I only remember my first kiss – all the way home – all through dinner.

'Davey, are you okay? You look a bit flushed.' Mom touches my forehead with her palm. 'You don't seem to have a fever. I'll give you some vitamin C just in case.' I have no idea what we ate for dinner.

'What is it with the goofy smile? The two of you are not going to give Ms Roux any hassles, are you?' I do not even mind Perfect Amelia's unfair accusation.

'No, I'm just happy.' I cannot wipe the smile from my face.

YEAR 3, MONTH 3, WEEK 10

GREENIE NO MORE

Captain David Zacharias Log

STARDATE 73638.21 LOG ENTRY 221

Finally, the orientation is done. We have earned our place at Weston High and can now wear the school tie and matching shoes. Weston High won the Revue trophy for the third year in a row. It was a close race, Weston winning by only ten points.

1. *Music lessons are fun again. I enjoy practising with Adam. He wants every note to be perfect but does not forget that it is about the music, as Ms Roux said.*
2. *I'm nervous about meeting Jennie – I don't know what to say. All I can think about is the kiss.*

On Monday, everything that could go wrong goes wrong. I should just have gotten back in bed and stayed there.

'Hey, your time is up. Get out of the bathroom.' I bang on the door to get my point across. 'Mom! Mom, Amelia is making me late – she's still in the bathroom. Tell her to get out. I'm going to be late. Moooom!'

'Heavens, Davey, what is with all the noise? Why are you not dressed yet? You should get up when I call you.' Mom's temper is also frayed at the edges.

'Because Miss Perfect is still in the bathroom. It's not my fault.'

'Amelia, please, we talked about this. Your brother also needs to use the bathroom. Open the door right now.' Mom rattles the handle but still no answer. 'Amelia, honey, are you okay?'

'What's wrong? Who's in the bathroom?' Mom and I turn to look at a neatly dressed Amelia, her long blond hair in a ballet bun on top of her head with a single curl artfully draped in front of her ear, backpack in her hand, ready for school.

'You locked the door on purpose to make me late!'

'I did not. The door is open. I even left the window open to let out the steam and wiped the mirror.' She reaches over to open the door. It does not budge. 'Mom, I didn't lock the door. Remember, I told you there is something wrong with the lock. I did not lock it after last time – I just put the little chair in front of the door.'

'I'll go get the key – maybe it is just stuck. Davey, just use the guest bathroom.'

'But all my stuff is here. I don't have a toothbrush, a towel, or my soap. I must use my soap; otherwise, my skin itches.'

'David Zacharias Miller, get yourself into that bathroom right now. Not a single word. I've had it with you this morning. Now.' Mom gives me her I-take-no-prisoner look, and I wisely beat a retreat. I finish at lighting speed, avoiding soap altogether. On my way back, both women are staring at the door. It seems the key has broken off in the lock. I silently tiptoe past them.

In the kitchen, the oats porridge has burned. It stinks badly; I dump the mess in the bin and open the window. Then I drop two used teabags in the burned pot and add water. I'm still busy putting breakfast together when Mom and Amelia enter the kitchen.

'Oh dear, I forgot the oats. It must have burned to a crisp. What are you going to have for breakfast now?'

'It's okay. I've made some muesli with fruit and yoghurt.' I hold out the bowl for Amelia to take to the table. It slips from my hand, yoghurt and muesli go flying. All over the floor, the cupboards, my shoes, my pants ...and Perfect Amelia.

'David Miller!'

'I did not do it on purpose! It slipped – it was an accident!'

'You are lying!'

'I'm not. I was trying to help. Mom, it was an accident. I promise...' I feel tears burning my eyes. 'I didn't do it on purpose – I was trying to help. I'm sorry.'

'Okay, Davey, no need to cry.'

'Mom, how can you take his side? He did it on purpose because of the bathroom door.' Amelia is furiously wiping at her shoes with a paper towel, trying to get rid of the gooey mess.'

'Amelia, I'm not taking sides. That is going to need a wet cloth. Leave your shoes and get changed. I don't want to hear it – go.'

'Why are you wearing your fat clothes?' Khanyi is waiting in the kitchen.

'David, are you trying my patience today? Please put on your new pants – you look ridiculous. Where did you find those pants?' Mom is going to explode when she hears the answer.

'They are from last year. My new pants are still in the sewing room. The seam on the one is out, and the other one's zip is broken.'

The wet cloth hits the wall above the sink and slips down to hide below. Khanyi grabs his muffin and seeks safety on the front stoep. Amelia flattens herself against the wall when Mom grabs me by the arm and marches me to the sewing room. My protest dies a silent death when I see the fire burning in her eyes. She yanks the drawer open. 'Hold this.' Mom hands me scissors and a roll of double-sided tape we use on gifts. She finds the pants that need seaming and spreads them on the work surface. 'Cut me a five-centimetre piece and stick it here.' We work in absolute silence – Mom points, I stick. When both legs are done. Mom turns and walks out of the room. 'Five minutes. Then I leave for school, and if you're not ready, you can walk.'

I change in a minute flat, grab my shoes, and run for the door. Someone has put my backpack and lunch bag next to the front door. The car is idling at the gate when I rush down the steps in socks. Khanyi opens the back door, and I dive in. It's a very quiet drive to Weston Primary. Khanyi slips from the car, and we continue. Mom pulls away without saying goodbye. I look at Amelia; she slowly nods her head – we will get an earful when Dad finds out that we have upset his wife and our mother.

I should have stayed in bed.

By first break, I'm bone tired. 'What's wrong with you today?' Max is puzzled by my strange behaviour. 'You did your homework – why did you not hand it in?' I've already been scolded twice for not handing in my homework – which somehow did not make it into my school bag on Sunday evening.

'I don't know. It's one of those days – the one with the wrong foot out of bed. Everything is just going wrong.' I barely finish talking when a girl falls over me. Only Max's quick action saves her from falling flat on the ground. Instead of being thankful, she lays into us.

'Are you stupid or something? Why are you sitting on the steps? Can't you see people walking here?'

'He's feeling sick, so he's sitting down.' Max tries to explain.

'Then take him to the nurse's office. Do you really have to be told everything?' We watch her hurry away.

'Might not be a bad idea, you know?'

'What?'

'Stay in the nurse's office. You seem to attract a lot of trouble today.'

'Won't they call my parents? Mom is already in a bad mood – I'd rather not take the chance.'

'Don't tell the nurse you are sick. Just say you have a headache and want to lie down for a bit.'

'David Miller. You are all grown up. My, my, my. And you have lost so much weight.' The school nurse is none other than Ms Merry with the purple bird hat from church. 'Are you feeling sick? Must I call your mom?'

'No, Ms Merry. I have a headache. I just want to lie down for a bit. I'll be okay in a while.' I hope Max is right and she believes me.

'Of course – you look a bit pale. Come in. Your sister is already here.

'My sister? Amelia is here?'

'Yes, she had a slight accident. We had to put in a stitch or two. I'm sure she won't mind you sharing the room. The other patient has a bit of an upset tummy.' Ms Merry does not wait for an answer. She opens the door. 'Amelia, dear, your brother is here. Can he come in?'

'Davey is here. Is he okay?'

'Yes, dear – he has a headache and is a bit pale. You don't mind, do you? Davey, you can lie down here. No need to take off your shoes; there is a plastic cover. Scoot down, and I'll put the blanket over you. Cripes, there goes that kid again. Let me go check on him.'

'What happened to your hand?' I ask. Amelia is sitting up,

cradling her hand covered in a white bandage. 'Why did you have to get stitches? How many did you get?'

'I cut my finger when I did a dissection in biology. The bleeding won't stop, and Ms Merry put in two stitches. She is more capable than she sounds and looks. What's wrong with you?'

I'm sticking to Max's story. 'I have a headache.'

'Hmm, I'll be quiet then.' She settles back against the pillows with a knowing smile and closes her eyes.

'Why are you laughing?'

'I'm sharing one of your adventures.'

'This is not an adventure – I have a headache.'

'Mmm, an escapade then. I like it.'

I decide to ignore her. 'Stop that – I can hear you giggling.'

'Hey, little brother, time to wake up. We need to get back to class.' I must have fallen asleep.

'How's the hand?'

'Not so bad. A bit sore now that the local is wearing off. The eighth period is going to start soon – which subject do you have?'

'Double Maths with Kaiser. I'm going to be in trouble. I left all my homework at home.'

'No wonder you have a headache. You only have to hang in there for four more periods. See you at practice.' The shrill ringing of the bell cuts her off; she waves and takes the stairs to the second floor. With a sigh, I find my way to Maths class.

I'm plagued by a hollow feeling in my stomach all through Thursday. I'm nervous about meeting Jennie again. Today will be the first time after the kiss. It's all I can think about and I'm glad for sports practice to take my mind off things. Especially since

I'm suddenly the replacement 200-metre runner for the under-14s. Number one fell off his bike, number two had flu, and the reserve has a stomach bug that he cannot shake. Max kindly volunteered my participation in the 200 and the relay.

When I reach the corner where we usually meet up, there is no sign of Jennie. I feel relieved and disappointed at the same time. Since there is still time, I decide to wait while trying out Mom's newly created orange, ginger, lemongrass and basil water infusion. Maybe next time, she should not add the basil.

'I was hoping that you had some more water.' Jennie has shown up, her face red and sweaty.

'I must look a mess.' She pushes back the strands of hair escaping from her braid. 'We had track practice, and I had to win. No way I'm going to lose to that snooty, pinched-face, pain-in-the-butt Melinda. Why did you drink all the water?'

'I didn't – here is yours.' I take out a stainless steel water bottle from my backpack. 'It still has ice cubes in it. I hope you like orange and ginger. Mom is coming up with new combinations all the time. It has basil in it too.'

'Thank you, thank you! Anything is good. I'm so thirsty.' I watch her press the cold bottle against her face and neck in an effort to cool down.'

'Did you win?' I can't remember ever seeing competitive Jennie before.

She gives me a fierce look, wiping her mouth before answering. 'Of course. It's my mission to put her in second place. She'll never get the first place as long as I'm there. She even came second in the ballet exam.'

'Why do you hate her so much?'

'Do you remember Lily, the girl from the library? You helped her with Maths.'

'Yes.' I remember the too-quiet, too-thin, blonde second grader from the library. The silent way she would share my lunch. I sometimes wonder about her, especially when I have mini frittatas for lunch. 'Is she okay? Did something happen to her?'

'She's not at school anymore.' She must have seen something on my face. 'No, nothing bad – she's living with her aunt. She's okay. Ellie's mom knows Lily's aunt and says Lily is okay. She has even started doing ballet again.'

'So, what did this Melinda do to Lily?' I don't even know this girl and I hate her already.

'Lily used to take ballet lessons with us. She is very good – like ballerina good. But her dad started to drink after her mom left. Sometimes he would show up at class all drunk and horrid. One time, Madam had to get security to remove him. It took four of them to get him out of the class. He was shouting. It was so loud. We were all scared and felt bad for Lily. However, prune-face Melinda started to say all these bad things about her. When Lily didn't get a good grade for the exam, she told her that she didn't belong in class and was an embarrassment to the ballet school. Lily cried so much and didn't come back to class at all. My mission ever since is to never ever let Melinda win at anything. She will always be second.' Her fierce expression reminds me of Sunny. I don't think it would be good for anyone to cross the Chen sisters. Jennie can't stop laughing when I tell her.

It's Friday afternoon, and anyone walking into my room would be shocked by the sight of three boys doing homework. It was Khanyi's proposal – doing homework together on Fridays, then it's out of the way and the parents are off our backs. We usually rotate between Adam's and my room since Khanyi's book-littered room is best for short visits. Even though it is neat, there is still no place to sit and do homework.

'This is an oxymoron.' I indicate the three of us.

'Lift up your book. I can't see what you have written.'

'No, Adam, I mean us – boys doing homework on a Friday afternoon is like an oxymoron.'

'There is no oxymoron in that sentence. Remember x and y go together. Ms Emmy says it is like awfully good, bad luck, or soft rock. Like that. You will have to try again.'

'I mean the situation – us three doing homework on Friday.'

'I'm sure many kids are doing homework on a Friday afternoon.' Khanyi putting in his two cents. 'You will need to read more books. How many have you read this year?'

'You only read magazines!'

'Still more than you. And I've read a travel book. Fess up; how many?'

'C'mon, Davey – you must have read three by now? You said you liked the one about the space pirates.'

'Two. You said one per month, so I'm on the third book. I'm on schedule! Finish your homework. It's nearly four, and it's already getting dark just after six.'

'Yes, be quick – I don't want Mommy to be mad again. She is acting weird too. Mommy bought stacks of medicines, masks, and sanitiser. Even Panado and lemon stuff and toilet paper, lots of toilet paper. It was not even on special – she says it must be done.'

'My mother too,' says Khanyi. 'She bought bread, flour, macaroni and stocked up the grocery cupboard with cans and spices. It's four o'clock. Pack up, let's go!'

When they race downstairs for our bike ride, I open the cupboard in my room and survey the neat rows of shampoo, toothpaste, deodorant, and body wash that have appeared. Seems my mom is also stocking up for something.

YEAR 3, MONTH 3, WEEK 11

LIKE AN APOCALYPSE MOVIE

Captain David Zacharias Log

STARDATE 73657.51 LOG ENTRY 222

1. *Find out what Mom and Dad are hiding. I'm pretty sure Perfect Amelia knows what is going on.*
2. *I need to decide if I want to play rugby… Big H wants to start the games in the park.*
3. *I've lost more weight. The gym must be helping. I'm saving to buy a long-sleeved sports shirt for the winter – it's grey and red with tiny pink triangles. I'm sure Amelia will approve of the colour.*

On Saturday, Dad drops me and Max off at his house after gym. Even Miss Perfect looks suitably impressed with the glass and concrete structure looming behind the many-meters-high wall and a gate with black and gold ironwork. Mom was totally against me visiting Max at home. She keeps saying this is not a good time to visit other people. She reluctantly agreed after talking to Max's grandmother.

'No need to drive in, Mr Miller,' says Max. 'We can go in through the small gate. Unless you wish to meet Babi.'

'No thanks, Max. A bit sweaty and smelly after the gym. Davey?'

'Yes, Dad, I know. I'll be on my best behaviour.' Max pulls me from the car.

'No worries, Mr Miller. I'll look after Davey.' He presses the remote, and a section of the enormous gate silently swings open 'Hurry, I'm hungry. Babi is cooking today.' I follow him through the gate and step into a different world. It is just like the house and gardens in the magazines Khanyi loves. The ones with manicured lawns, hidden arbours, gravel pathways, and garden art. We run all the way up to the house, a good hundred metres from the gate. At the side door, I wave to Dad.

'Wow, you must be super-rich.'

'The parents are. Mikhail too. He holds patents on his inventions. Me, not so much. I only have my pocket money.'

'What is a patent?'

'It is like a licence for his inventions, and people pay to use it. Some of his inventions are used by the military and NASA. Let's go shower – else Babi will throw us out of the kitchen. I hope you like *syrniki*. Babi promised to make it, especially for your visit.'

'I have no idea what that is.'

'It is like a cheese fritter but made with Russian cottage cheese. Babi makes her own cottage cheese. She says the shops are no good. We eat it with honey, sour cream, and jam. You can eat yours with yoghurt. I know you like yoghurt.'

Max's bedroom is HUGE. It looks like a flat with a balcony. Even his clothes have a room of their own. Max opens a door and pushes me into yet another room.

'You can use Mikhail's shower; he won't mind. I've put out towels and soap for you. The shower will start once you close the door. Just wave your hand in front of the red button to warm the water. This was my idea. Mikhail helped me set it. A pre-programmed automated shower. Cool, huh?'

'Super cool.'

After a quick shower, we rush downstairs for lunch. Max throws his arms around a woman standing in front of a fridge that covers half the kitchen wall. Everything in this house is super-sized. 'Babi, meet Davey.'

'Easy there. Always in a rush.' She reminds me of Grandma Edith, tall and thin. But where my grandma comes across as cold and aloof, this woman is warm. She smiles, hugging Max back; friendly blue eyes invite me in, and she extends her arm. 'Ah, Davey, Max's best friend. I've heard so much about you. It feels like I already know you. Welcome to our home. You can call me Babi. Come, sit. Lunch is ready.' She tries to push her runaway grey-black hair back into the bun, but it escapes again, dancing around her face. 'I've made *syrniki*. It's Max's favourite. If you do not like it, there is also fresh rye bread, fruit and cheese. Help yourself.'

I bite into a crunchy, warm, golden *syrniki*. The slightly sour kick is unexpected. The inside is somewhat dry and creamy, like a baked cheesecake.

'Try it with yoghurt and honey. I like it with sour cream and peach jam. Babi likes blueberries.'

It turns out I like my *syrniki* with three citrus marmalade. After breakfast, Babi chases us outside. 'Play outside, Max. The sunshine is good for you – winter is coming. Go, go, go.'

'I'm going, see in the sun.' Max opens his arms wide and spins on one leg in the sunshine. 'Let's go biking!'

I follow Max to the back of the house, and when we round the corner, I have to pick up my jaw from the grass. 'You have a bike track in your backyard?'

'Yes. Mikhail needed it for experiments. I use it as a pump track. Blue, green or red?'

'Red, I think. Adam will love this! He won't believe it when I tell him.'

When I turn around, Max is pulling a red bike from the shed, a red and white checked helmet swinging from the handlebars. 'See if the seat is okay. I'll get some knee guards and gloves. Coming down hurts a lot. But it's still fun.' Max disappears into the shed again.

Properly suited up, I follow Max, riding on a green bike, around the track. He shows me how to use my body and momentum to generate speed and not by pedalling. After a few tries, I make a perfect jump and ride my bike on the back wheel. Thanks to the padding, no serious damage is sustained when I mess up.

'Davey?'

'Mmm?' I'm lying on the soft grass. The warm sunshine is making me lazy and drowsy. I need a rest after all that biking.

'You are not angry with me? Are you?'

I open one eye and look at Max, sitting with his arms crossed over his knees. 'Angry? Why?'

'I told Babi that you are my best friend. I know it's not true – Adam is your best friend. And Khanyi.'

I cannot help smiling. 'I don't think Khanyi would like to be called my best friend. We are friends because Adam wants to be friends. I didn't like him in the beginning, but he's okay now. I don't think he likes me much. Adam is my best friend. People sometimes think he is like my little brother. I must keep him out of trouble.' I sit up. 'Max, I want to be your friend. I never had a friend my age. School isn't so bad when you are there. And Legs too.'

Max holds out his hand. 'Let's shake on it. Friends for now. I'll work on being a best friend.'

'Good. Me too.'

After a delicious supper of Jamie's Popeye Toast, all green and eggy with Tannie Kotie's vine tomatoes, Dad says to gather for a Family Meeting. When Dad starts talking about the Coronavirus and COVID-19, a dangerous virus that is making people very sick all around the world so sick that they can die, my heartrate picks up. My world slows down and stops. It feels like my head is floating away; I'm cold and hot, cold and hot. 'Dad, what if Adam gets sick? Is Adam going to die?'

'No. Children do not seem to be affected by the virus. So far, it has only been adults who have been infected. If you follow the health protocols, you and Adam will be fine. From Monday onwards, you shall wear a mask to school and regularly wash your hands with sanitiser whenever you touch surfaces used by others. You must also practice social distancing.'

'I don't understand.'

Mom explains about one metre apart. Not to visit Adam to keep him safe. Dad says our masks must cover our mouth and nose. Amelia talks about not touching anything, especially your face. A numbness settles over me. Their voices flow over and around me.

'Can I be excused?'

'David, come here.' I get up and walk over to where Dad is sitting at the head of the table. 'David, look at me. We will be okay because we will take care of each other. We are going to keep each other safe. We are going to believe that God will keep us safe and protected. What does Father Bosinio always say?'

'Have faith.'

'You believe that don't you?' I nod my head, but inside I'm shaking. 'Then have some faith that all will be well.'

'I'm still scared. Are you going to die?'

'Oh, Munchkin.' Mom's hug is warm around my back, and she gives me a kiss on the cheek. I look into Dad's blue eyes. He is not smiling.

Back in my room, I videocall the other two on Whatsapp. 'Did you hear about the Coronavirus?'

It seems that the news of the Coronavirus has not affected Adam. 'I have a secret! Mommy says I cannot tell you because I'm a good friend.'

'Aren't you scared that you'll get sick?'

'I'm already sick, dummy. Mommy says now everyone will be in quarantine, not only me. Like the whole world. I have a secret that you don't know…'

'Khanyi?'

'Davey, it's going to be okay. Mother says if we follow the rules, we will stay healthy. Look what I have. It's like the masks Ms Megan gives us when visiting Adam. You must wear it like this.' Khanyi demonstrates the correct way of wearing a mask. 'And you cannot touch it. At all. You must wash your hands with sanitiser before taking it off.' He measures out three drops of the sanitiser, washes his hands, and then carefully removes the mask by pulling the white strings. 'See like that. Adam – did you even see anything while jumping all over the place? I have even better news than your secret.'

'Is not. I have the best news.'

'A secret is not news. You are not supposed to tell people you have a secret.'

'It's still news.'

'Is not!'

'Is so!'

I do not understand these two. Are they not afraid of the virus? People are dying! I should have called Max, but Dad has not approved his email address yet. 'STOP! If you are going to fight, I'm logging off.' They give me similar surprised looks and quieten down.

'Sheeze, no need to shout like that. You sound like Mother.'

'Yes, he does.'

'What's your news Khanyi?'

'You can meet my gogos on Monday. They are coming to stay with us while there is Corona.'

'Both of them? I can see both of them?' Adam can't believe his luck. He finally gets to meet the famous identical gogos.

'Wow. Isn't your mom angry anymore? What time will they be here on Monday?'

'That is the best news of all. They'll be here at six in the morning. You can meet them before school. Isn't that fantastic! My gogos are coming!' Now it is Khanyi doing a happy dance. 'I hope Corona stays for a long time. Davey, you must wear your new pants and shirt for my gogos. You also, Adam. I can't wait for tomorrow!'

That evening while watching the warm glow cast by the friendship light in the window, I think about Max alone in the big house with only his grandma. His parents and Mikhail are never there. Even though he always looks happy, he's lonely. When Mom and Dad came to pick me up, his smile looked so sad. He held Babi's hand the whole time. She was hugging him when I looked back. I wonder if his parents will come home now.

YEAR 3, MONTH 3, WEEK 12

A STATE OF DISASTER

Captain David Zacharias Log

STARDATE 73676.81 LOG ENTRY 223

1. *On 15 March 2020, the President of South Africa, Cyril Ramaphosa, declared a national state of disaster. He announced that nobody could travel outside the country, and even travelling between provinces was a no-no. He also said that schools would close from 18 March 2020. The president said this is necessary as the virus is deadly and people are dying.*
2. *I don't want Mom and Dad to die. I don't want anyone to die.*
3. *I'm scared that Adam is going to die. I want him to stay in his special room until this virus goes away.*

I wake up from a horrible nightmare in the early hours of Monday, all twisted up, sweating and crying. When rational thought returns, I do something I haven't done in a long time. I take my pillow and duvet and head for Amelia's room.

'Amelia?'

'I'm awake. Are you okay? What is wrong? Get in; it's cold.'

In two seconds flat, I've made my bed and snuggled down. 'Why are you awake? Did you have a nightmare too?'

'No… I'm just thinking. What was the nightmare about?'

'The Last Ship. They didn't want me on the ship because I had Corona. All of you left. Even Adam, Khanyi and stupid Bernie were leaving on the ship.'

'Having Bernie in any dream is a nightmare.' I'm glad she sees the funny in the nightmare. 'Do you remember how angry Mom was when she found out you were watching the Last Ship with us?'

'I didn't find it scary then. I wanted to be Captain Tom Chandler. He was like a superhero.'

In the dark, I can hear Amelia giggle. 'You told Mom that we should move to Simon's Town. You said you want to go to Navy School.'

'You told me I must learn to swim first.' We fell silent again. 'Do you think they will find a cure as they did in the series?'

'Of course they will. We must just take care until then. Go to sleep; it's already Monday.' I fell asleep, listening to Amelia breathing.

Monday, mindful of Khanyi's instructions, I dress in my best-fitting school shirt and pants, making sure my tie is not crooked and that my blazer is spotless. Even my shoes are shining. I want to make a good impression on the gogos. They are already at the gate by the time we leave for school. The gogos, one in beautiful orange-brown and the other in green and yellow traditional print dresses with matching masks, are waiting with Khanyi and Remo. 'This is my Gogo Simi, and this is Gogo Nonhla. *Igama lakhe ngu-Amelia futhi ungu Davey.*'

I've been practising; taking a deep breath, I greet them in Zulu. '*Sanibonani mama. Ninjani?*'

Gogo Nonhla, with a twinkle in her eye, greets me back. '*Ngiyaphila, wena unjani?*'

'Ngiyaphila.' I've reached the end of my Zulu language skills, but the arrival of a masked Adam with his mom in tow luckily picked up the conversation.

'I'm Adam. *Sanibonani.* Are you twins? Are you really identical? How old are you? Did it take you long to get here? Are you tired?' His mom silences Adam by placing a hand over his mask.

'I'm sorry. He always does that.'

Gogo Simi, in the orange-brown dress, says something to Khanyi that makes him smile, and Remo laughs out loud.

'Gogo Simi says you remind her of a little monkey. You talk so fast and want to know so many things at once.'

The Coronavirus is on everyone's lips at school. It's the only thing they talk about and the school holidays starting earlier. 'Are your parents coming back to South Africa now?' I ask Max.

'No. They are going to stay at Oxford with Mikhail. Father is going to help with research.'

'And your mom?'

'She's looking after him – he is a bit of a scatterbrain. Don't worry so much, Davey. I'll be fine. Babi is staying, and Auntie May is also back. You haven't met her yet – she is sweet and has been our housekeeper forever. Babi says that Auntie May's husband will also stay at the house since their kids are overseas and are not planning to return. He loves gardening as much as your Tannie Kotie.'

'I'll ask Dad to add you to my contact list then we can WhatsApp. I don't think Mom is going to let me go anywhere.'

'Can't you do it yourself? I'll show you how.'

'Not if I want to keep my electronic privileges. My mom freaked out the last time I emailed someone not on the list. Dad will do it this evening, adding you and Legs.' I'm hoping Dad will also add Jennie to the list. Perhaps I should ask Dad if I can add my friends to my contact list now that I'm in high school. It never bothered me before since I had no friends.

Mom was waiting on the stoep, all masked up when we arrived home. 'Leave your shoes outside the door. Also, your school bags. I'll wipe them down. Use the guest bathroom to wash your hands and leave your clothes in the hamper. Your blazer on the hanger – I'll hang it in the sun. Only then can you go up to your rooms. There is a separate basket for your masks.'

'What am I supposed to wear if I take off my school clothes?'

'I've put out clothes for you, Davey. Go.'

'Mom, is this not a bit of overkill? Was this Dad's idea?' Lucky it's Amelia asking and not me.

'Tannie Kotie.' Of course it was her; who else would think up such a ridiculous scenario? Turns out, when she was younger, she worked with Doctors Without Borders and knows about epidemics and quarantine. I'm just glad that there are no white towels to be seen anywhere.

That evening Dad handed out our holiday chores. No sitting around. I did not moan about the long list since Dad added Max, Legs and Jennie without any comments. He also bought home four computer monitors. He set up two in his home office. The other two he put up in Mom's workroom, which is now strangely devoid of anything remotely related to needlework and party goods. 'Dad, why are you putting these here?'

'Just setting up some workspace for when we need it. Plug that cable in here. Do the same to the other. Now, let's tidy it up with the cable ties.'

We listen with morbid fascination as the COVID-19 figures for the last 24 hours are announced. As of the morning of 18 March 2020, South Africa has 116 confirmed cases of COVID-19. An increase of 31 new cases from yesterday's announcement.

'If the figures keep rising like this, we will go into lockdown.' Mom shakes her head. 'If people just follow the rules, all will be okay.'

'Mom, what is lockdown? Are they going to put people in jail?'

'No, Munchkin, it is more like a countrywide quarantine. It's a policy that restricts people from moving around. They must stay home and not go out.'

'What if you are on holiday? Must you stay there until the lockdown is done?'

'I suppose so since they do not want people to travel. It is time to leave for school. Switch off the radio. Where's your sister?'

Just as I'm reaching to switch off, the newsreader reports the number of cases in Italy as 35 898, an increase of more than 5 000 cases in 24 hours and the total number of deaths as 2 503. An increase of 16%.

'Mom, do you think Father Bosinio is okay?' The Father left for Rome at the beginning of February.

'I'm sure he is. Father Tilly would have said something in church. Get a move on; Khanyi is waiting at the gate. Remember to wear your mask and sanitise.' Mom is pushing me out the door. 'Amelia, Davey is leaving. You are going to be late.'

Too soon, the last day of school is done, and I have to say goodbye to Max until school starts in April again. I did not even get to see Jennie. I hope she is okay. Some kids call the Coronavirus the Chinese virus and blame the Chinese people. Wentworth even said that all Chinese people must be deported. Dad says that is a racist statement and it is very bad to oversimplify and blame the Chinese people. I feel bad for Jennie, maybe I should WhatsApp her to hear if she is okay.

The first day of the school holiday does not feel like a holiday. I even wake up at seven and can't get back to sleep. I decide to investigate what Mom is making for breakfast.

'You are up early? Is something wrong? Are you feeling sick?'

'Nooo, just hungry. What are we having for breakfast?'

Mom switches off the radio. 'I'm making Jamie's one-cup pancakes. It is super easy. Want to help?'

'Pancakes for breakfast? With cinnamon sugar – that cannot be healthy.'

'We are going to add berries and yoghurt – no sugar. And if you give me a hand, we can grate apple and pear together for Dad.'

'Okay – I'll grate the apple but not the squishy pear. Do we have to grate it?'

In no time at all, we are done with four flapjack-size pancakes for everyone. They really are fifteen-minute pancakes. Mom says these babies are less than 300 kilojoules, so they are getting a healthy tick in my book, and the holidays are off to a good start.

Around eleven, the phone rings and after a few minutes of muted conversation, Mom calls me downstairs. 'That was Ms Megan. Could you please take Adam for a bike ride but not to the park? He is being difficult.' Mom has barely finished talking when the gate bell sounds. 'I'll let him know you are on your way. Stay away from people and keep your mask on.'

'Hey, what did you do for your mom to kick you out?'

'Nothing. I didn't do anything. Where is Khanyi? Will he come too?'

'I don't know. Let's ask.' While we wait for Khanyi, I grill Adam. 'Your mom said you are being difficult. You must have done something?'

Adam is playing innocent. 'I didn't do anything. Mommy is being mean. I was just asking questions.'

'Yo, where are we going?' Khanyi comes to a standstill by spinning on his back wheel. Today he is dressed in red Adidas track pants and a two-tone black and white graphic tee with a half-bear, half-robot print. Red sneakers complete his look. Our discerning fashionista is looking sharp. Sometimes I wish I could dress like that.

'How did you get out of the house? I thought your mom would lock you in the special room until the Coronavirus goes away.'

'His mom kicked him out.'

'Didn't. She said to get out of her hair.'

'You must have made her mad. What did you do?' Khanyi is not moving until he gets his answer. He folds his arms, ready to wait.

Adam, seeing that he is going nowhere, spills the beans. 'Mommy said everyone was going into quarantine, not only me. So, I wanted to know why I had to stay in the special room? She should give Uncle the special room. Mommy got so angry – her face was all red. Then she told me I can go biking with Davey.'

'You have an uncle living with you?' I haven't seen anyone besides Adam and his mom.

'Where did he come from? Do we know him?'

'It's a secret. I can't tell you.' No matter how hard we try, we cannot get a single word out of Adam about the strange uncle living with them.

Racing around the block wearing a mask is suffocating and tiring. After a while, we give up and just cruise around the neighbourhood until hunger drives us home. When I told the two to leave their shoes, helmets and protective gear on the stoep, they thought I was nuts. That was even *before* I told them that we must also wash our hands and faces in the little guest bathroom before eating. I explained that on school days Mom would sanitise our school backpacks, and after changing out of our school clothes we must wash our hands and faces before we could go upstairs.

'I hope your mom will not tell my mother about this washing rule. The mask-wearing and sanitising is bad enough, but I'm not sharing a small bathroom with five women. That is why I have my own bathroom.'

Adam finds it very funny that Khanyi is the only male in the home. 'You are the only boy; that makes you the man of the house. Must you take out the rubbish and kill the spiders?'

'No. Mother and Keeya take out the wheelie-bins – they are too heavy for me. Remo doesn't want us to kill the spiders. She usually starts crying, so we just set them free. Are we clean enough? Can we eat now? I'm hungry.'

My stomach agrees loudly with that suggestion. The smells coming from the kitchen are a gravitational force pulling us in. There is definitely some bacon involved.

YEAR 3, MONTH 3, WEEK 13

LOCKDOWN LEVEL 5

Captain David Zacharias Log

STARDATE 73696.11 LOG ENTRY 224

1. *On Monday, 23 March 2020, President Cyril Ramaphosa announced that a 21-day national lockdown shall start at midnight on 26 March 2020 and continue until 16 April 2020.*
2. *For the first time, I'm not excited about a longer school holiday. I've even started on my homework.*
3. *The first death in South Africa from COVID-19 was reported on 27 March 2020.*
4. *I'm worried about Father Bosinio and Adam. Why is Adam not afraid?*

On Sunday, 22 March 2020, South Africa had 274 confirmed cases of COVID-19. An increase of 34 from yesterday. Most of these cases are in Gauteng, with a total of 132. Still no deaths in South Africa. Maybe we are stronger than most. The newsreader gives the numbers for Italy. On Saturday, 793 Italians had died from the Coronavirus, the most in a single day anywhere in the world. Another 651 Italians died on Sunday.

Their total number of infections is 59 439. I don't think Father Bosinio is safe anymore. I wish he had stayed in South Africa. Every time I open my mail, with no answer from him, it feels like long cold fingers reach out, lock around my heart and squeeze it until I have no breath left. My stomach also hurts really bad. Maybe today he'll message.

At church, everyone is speculating whether the president will talk this evening and if he would announce the lockdown. Others say it would be longer than fourteen days since it takes five to seven days for a person to get sick. When Father Tilly asks for a moment of silent prayer, I pray for Father Bosinio, Grandpa Heinz, and Grandma Edith in Germany. I open my eyes. Dad prays silently next to me, only his lips moving. I catch sight of his hands folded together, his knuckles showing white. I put my hand on top of his. He doesn't open his eyes; he just takes my hand. We don't let go until the service ends.

Monday the 23rd is a warm autumn day – perfect holiday weather. Mom is making omelettes for breakfast. I chop the oxheart tomatoes while Amelia halves the white button mushrooms. Mom adds the basil and parsley to the egg mixture, whisks it together and then pours it into the pan. It doesn't take long for the eggs to set, and Mom adds the tomatoes, mushrooms, and baked beans.

'Why are you adding baked beans?'

'It's a Mexican omelette, Davey. It's spicy with a jalapeño or two.'

'Taking risks, I see. Did you take out the pips?'

'I did.' Amelia is also watching the eggs changing colour. 'It's nearly done. Are you going to flip it?'

'Mom shakes her head and hands the spatula to Amelia. 'You do the honours.'

The first one was a bit of a flop, but the second and third ones turn out great. Next time I'm in charge of flipping. Mexican is not so spicy. I like it.

The rest of the day is filled with online games, biking and a visit to the gym. Max and I have a good workout, and Amelia says she'll treat us to smoothies at the Kauai shop while waiting for Dad. This time I pick the Peanut Butter Bomb, which is super delicious, smooth and peanutty. Max wants to try the pink Strawberry Stinger. It does taste very strawberry-ish. Amelia's is a concoction called All the Greens. It is very green – so gross. Max says it tastes like green apples and other nameless things. We are joking around when Amelia receives a WhatsApp: a notice that the president would talk at 20:00 on national TV about South Africa's actions against the virus. People begin to rush from the gym to get home before the broadcast starts.

When Dad picks us up, he is even more quiet than usual. At Max's house, he stops and turns around in his seat; he is not smiling, looking all serious. 'Max, stay safe and call us if there are any problems or if you need help. Don't go out unnecessarily.' Max's parents did not come home when the state of disaster was declared.

'Don't worry, Mr Hank. We're all set up for online orders and deliveries. And Miss May and her husband are staying with us. We'll be okay.'

Mom is waiting on the stoep with sanitiser and towels for everyone when we arrive home. 'Dinner in 30 minutes. Go shower. I want dinner done and the kitchen cleaned before the president talks.'

I rush through my shower in record time and join Mom in the kitchen. Dad is at the kitchen island, slicing tomatoes. 'Dad, Max says the president will put the country on lockdown. He says we will not be able to go anywhere. Is that true, Dad?'

'That's the meaning of lockdown, but let's wait for the president to talk before getting all worked up and worried. Here, put the tomatoes on the table and the white pepper too.'

We are all in the family room at eight, gathered around the TV. My usual place is the big chair next to Mom and Dad on the sofa. I hate these broadcasts that make me feel like I'm in an end-of-the-world movie; I have these mixed feelings of excitement and fear. I do not tell anyone this – they'll think I'm a drama queen. As expected, the president is delayed, and we check out all the jokes flying around on WhatsApp. The one I like best is a skeleton on a park bench that goes: Dude, you are very late.

The president opens his speech by thanking the people of South Africa. Then he starts to talk about rising infections, the strain on the medical services, not following the rules, and many other things. He pauses before announcing, '... *consequently, the National Coronavirus Command Council has decided to enforce a nationwide lockdown for 21 days with effect from midnight on Thursday, 26 March.*' I did not follow much after that. The president begins to explain about essential services, bans, etc.

'Dad, must we stay in the house the whole time? Can we go outside?'

'Yes, you can go outside, but you must stay in the erf. You need to stay within your family group and not visit other people. No going over to Adam or Khanyi.'

'Like the restraining order? Can I still visit Adam tomorrow? It's not the 26th yet?'

'No, Munchkin – let's hear what Ms Megan says before you go over. There is a lot to do and get ready before Friday. We must list what is needed and get to the shop early before it sells out.'

'I don't want to go to the shops. It's boring.'

'You're such a baby; if we all help, it will go faster. You take a list, and I take a list, and we can be in and out before it gets busy.' Amelia being perfect again.

'I don't wanna go.'

'David, that's enough. All of us must do our part. Hon, let me know what is not in stock, and I'll get it on my way back from Johannesburg. Perhaps you, Megan, Tan Kotie and Thandeka can split the shopping between you.'

'Tannie Kotie is already taking care of the fruit and vegetables…'

I grab the chance to slip away. I must talk to the others.

'Did you hear! Everyone will be in quarantine, but you don't have to stay in your room. You must stay in the house. The government is going to lock us in for 21 days. That is a very long time, like three Sundays.' Adam seems excited by the prospect of being locked in by the government.

'It is called lock*down*. Nobody is locking us in. It is like a new law that says we must stay at home. Mother has bought heaps of food and stuff, and we are going shopping tomorrow. I won't be able to go biking.' Unlike me, Khanyi is looking forward to shopping. 'Dad said I have to go.'

'Who is going biking with me? I want to go before locking in starts.'

'Maybe after shopping.'

'You'll be gone the whole day. What am I going to do? Why do you all have to go? This is not fair. I'm always left behind.'

Only after Khanyi and I heart-promise to go biking the moment we get home does Adam calm down, and we can make plans for the last days of freedom before 'locking in' starts.

I get to learn what essential goods are at breakfast the next day. 'Carly says that all the restaurants are closed, and shops cannot sell prepared food,' says Amelia. 'No pizzas, hamburgers, fish and chips, lemon and herb chicken. Even the bakeries are closed. What about those people who don't know how to cook?'

'Uncle Jo will starve.' I imagine Uncle Jo slowly getting thinner and thinner until he is too weak to do anything.

'Davey, please do not talk with food in your mouth. Uncle Jo will not starve. He can cook. He just chooses not to. Amelia, those items are not essential foods. We must get bread, meat, eggs and flour today before they sell out. The factories are closing too.'

'Only grocery stores selling essential products such as food and non-alcoholic beverages, animal food, electricity, airtime, hygiene, personal and cleaning products will be open. As well as pharmacies for medication and shops that sell fuel such as gas and coal will be open.' Amelia is reading from her phone. 'They are putting the whole country on a diet. Do sweets count as essential food?'

'We are not eating sweets, or biscuits or anything. I'm not getting fat again. Mom, you are not going to buy sweets, are you?'

'Amelia, no phones at the table. Davey, we are sticking to regular food.'

'Mom, we cannot even buy clothes. It says clothing retail is not an essential service.'

'Amelia, I'm sure we will survive if we do not buy clothes for 21 days. Put that phone away – last warning. I want to leave in 30 minutes.'

When we arrive at the shopping centre, I want to dive back into the car. It is madness, with people rushing everywhere, pulling, and pushing to get into the shops. Some people get aggressive, swearing, and shouting at security when instructed to wear masks. A woman starts to scream at the staff when she is told that some food articles are limited to three per customer. Mom suspected that would happen and gave me Tannie Kotie's shopping list. Most of the foods on the list are easy to find, but I have no idea where to find brewer's yeast.

'What are you looking for, baba?' One of the staff stocking the shelves has noted my confusion. I show him the list.'

'Shopping for Grandma. You are going to need the good stuff. Come with me. You want the dry or wet one?' He must have seen from the blank look that I have no idea what he is talking about. When we get to the fridge, he shakes his head. 'All gone.' He takes off skilfully, dodging shopping carts, baskets and irate customers. I jog after him, getting rammed by carts, stepped on, and someone even drops a bag of rice on my head. When we reach the baking goods, he hands me a green box with ten little packages. 'Here, this is good.' With my guide, we finish up the rest of the list. He then calls one of the cashiers and pushes and pulls me until we reach the front of the queue. Anyone that dares to complain is told, 'Grandma is waiting'. The cashier expertly rings up the stuff and shows me how to swipe the orange savings card we find inside the green and blue beaded purse.

'Thank you for helping me.'

'Next time you shop for Grandma online – 60 minutes fast and easy. I'll deliver for you.'

Too quick, the last days of freedom fly by. Our playing now has an unexpected urgency; we want to pack in as much as possible each day. Perhaps deep down, our primitive selves know that nothing will ever be the same. By eight, we are out biking, meeting up later to play a game of rugby sevens with Big H and the others in the park. Adam enjoys the faster game and cheers anyone on his way to the try line. When hunger drives us home, we sit outside on the stoep a metre apart, eating warm English muffins with thickly sliced red tomatoes and mozzarella cheese, chasing it down with a cup of Milo. It is only when the trees start casting long blue shadows on the street that we reluctantly return home. On the twenty-sixth, we find reasons to stay out longer. We ended up playing ball with Remo and Amelia under the streetlights. Eventually, Ms Megan comes outside and calls Adam home. The clang of the garden gate has a strange finality as if it knew we would only be allowed outside again after three long weeks.

Day 1 of lockdown. The newness of talking to each other over Microsoft Teams wears off fast, and boredom sets in. We can only play so many games before we start fighting instead of playing. Khanyi logs off to go watch a movie with his gogos. I lie on my bed, wondering what to do next. I'm not really in the mood to finish my homework. I've just dunked a beautiful shot in the hoop behind the door when it opens.

'I could have face-balled you. Why don't you ever knock?'

'No need – I knew you were playing. Let's go. It is time for exercise.' I stare at Perfect Amelia, all Energiser Bunny dressed in gym clothes.

'We're in lockdown. Why are you wearing gym clothes?' She looks nice in her dark blue, yellow, and pink outfit. Her hair is twisted up in a ballet bun.

'I know, silly. It's now time for exercise. I talked to Mom and Dad, and they agreed we should have a training schedule. It is now time for cardio – meet you in the garage. Get out of your pyjamas and put on your gym clothes.' She must have seen the I'm-not-going-anywhere look. 'I can ask Dad to come and explain.'

'Close the door on your way out. We are supposed to have a family meeting first. You cannot just set a schedule, and we have to agree. It's not fair.' But I'm already scrambling to get dressed. Best not to make Dad angry; there is not much space to hide.

This time around, I can keep up with the Energiser Bunny. I'm surprised that Mom is not missing a beat. Dad has always been fit, and he seems to enjoy the workout. When it is over, I take my rubbery legs upstairs. If we keep this up, I'll never gain weight again.

'Dad, are we going to have a family meeting about the new schedule?' It is midday, and Mom has prepared a vegetarian's dream lunch. Crispy toasted white bread with buttery smashed white beans, creamy green avocado, and red onion chopped into tiny bits for that peppery crunch. I've not yet made up my mind about beans, but I do know I like red beans more than white beans. The white beans are a bit blah.

'Davey, we discussed it on Monday night. Were you not listening?' Dad's blue eyes are pinning me in place. 'You did agree we need to set a daily programme. You mentioned homework. We all need to pull our weight in keeping the house and yard clean and neat.'

'No, Dad.' A frown creases his forehead. 'I mean, yes, Dad. It's just the cardio – are we only going to do cardio? Every day?'

'You must ask the person in charge of the exercise plan. Amelia?'

Amelia puts down her knife and fork and daintily wipes her mouth. 'I've read up about exercise plans…' I get a terrible feeling in my stomach; Mom also looks worried. 'We need to bring in variation in the training plan, like strength and agility training. I've borrowed some weights from Carly.'

'Weights? Are you sure?' Mom asks the question that has been burning on my tongue.

'Don't worry, Mom, they're only hand weights. The heaviest is five kilograms for Dad. The others are one, two and three kilograms. We are not bulking up; it's only strength training. We can practice five days a week with rest days in between. I thought it would help us fight COVID if we keep fit and healthy.' When she puts it like that, none of us can argue with her.

Later that evening, while drying the dishes, I checked out the lockdown family schedule that had appeared overnight on the pinboard in the kitchen. And there it is, 45 minutes set aside each day for exercise. Only Thursdays and Sundays are exercise-free. It seems I'm on yard duty tomorrow – raking leaves.

'What are you writing?' Adam is being a bit of a pest. His homework is done, but according to the Miller Lockdown Programme, I'm still in the homework period.

'I'm writing my journal for History. Mr De Wet says these are historic times, and we must record history. Our homework is to keep a diary, like Anne Frank during the Second World War. He says he does not want to read boring diaries; we must make them interesting and enjoyable. I'm keeping a journal like the captains in Star Trek; I call it Captain David Zacharias Log.'

'What do you write in it? Can you read a little bit for me? I want to know what you are writing; please – please – please…'

'Okay! I'll read you yesterday's log. I'm still busy with today's.'

Captain's log for Starship Zacharias

Stardate 27 March 2020 Entry 3-009

'How can it be entry three dash zero zero nine? Lockdown only started yesterday. It must be entry number two. Why did you name your Starship Zacharias?'

'It is entry three dash zero zero nine. It is the ninth day since the school closed on the eighteenth, and it is three because Starship Zacharias launched three years ago. Are you going to listen or moan about everything? This is my journal. I can write what I want.'

'You haven't told me why the starship is called Zacharias?'

'It is my second name, okay? I'm not calling it David. It sounds stupid. Mr De Wet said we must use our name. Can I read now?'

'I did not know your second name is Zacharias. Do you know what my second name is?'

'Yes. Sullivan. You told Grandpa Heinz when you first met him. You sounded just like your father when you said: I am Adrian Sullivan McKenzie the fourth. I remember it because Mom's surname was Sullivan before she married Dad. Do you have more questions, or can I read further?'

'You can read.' Adam is sulking.

Captain's log for Starship Zacharias

Stardate 27 March 2020 Entry 3-009

This is the second day since Starfleet Commander-In-Chief Cyril Ramaphosa ordered a Level 5 Lockdown.

Coronavirus Report

Captain David Miller of Starship Zacharias reports that all personnel are in good health.

There is still no report from Senior Officer Bosinio at Space Station Italy. Chief Engineer and Security Officer Miller to investigate and report.

Captain Heinz of Space Station Guten Morgen reported no cases present, and all are in good health.

Starfleet released the World Health Organisation report on 27 March 2020. There are 706 084 cases worldwide. The total number of deaths 29 400; this is 3 611 more than yesterday. An increase of 14%. Recoveries are at 100 000 plus cases. A 48-year-old woman is the first person to die in South Africa from the Coronavirus. South

Africa now has 1 170 confirmed cases. This is an increase of 243 from yesterday.

Chief Medical Officer Maximillian Shuler-Brown says the Oxford team is working on a vaccine. It will only be ready in twelve to eighteen months.

Operations Chief Bubbles Sullivan reports that all provisions taken on board on the 26th have been appropriately stored. Ration control is being implemented to ensure that food is available should we not be able to take on provisions after 21 April 2020. Horticulture Officer Kotie Klopper will supplement any food shortages from her food bank. Engineering Chief Miller reported the ship to be in good condition and submitted a maintenance schedule. Social Science Officer Amelia Perfecto has developed an extremely vigorous exercise schedule saying it would help with COVID-19 prevention.

End of Report

'Wow, that's so cool.' It seems Khanyi has come online while I was reading my journal. 'Are you doing it for fun?'

'No, it's History homework; we have to do a diary.' I explain the homework assignment to Khanyi.

'It sounds more fun than my memory project for English Lit. Let's all do a captain's log. We can have a captain's meeting each day and read each other's logs.'

'Come on Davey, say yes! I'll be Captain Adam from the Starship McKenzie. Khanyi, what are you going to call your starship?'

'I'll be Captain Mbuli from the Starship Lebombo.'

'Lebombo?' Adam has a pencil up his nose.

'Is that a river? Why name your starship after a river?'

Khanyi surprises us with one of his rare smiles. 'Eish, you know nothing. You should read magazines. Lebombo is the name of the Boeing 747 that flew over Ellis Park for the 1995

Rugby World Cup. I read it in the magazine they put on the plane for people to read. I asked the flight attendant, and she said it was okay if I wanted to keep the magazine since it was nearly the end of the month, and then they put in new magazines.' Khanyi proudly shows us a picture of a Boeing with the South African flag. 'See, there it says Lebombo. Mother promised to take me to the SAA Museum to see the real plane. Maybe you can come too.'

'We cannot go anywhere. We can only go after locking in. My starship has a good name too. It's named McKenzie, like my surname. But Miss Emmy says it is also the name of Sir Alexander, a great explorer who went to the Arctic. He walked right across North America. It is a good name for a starship. Uncle Jo and Aunt Mabel are on my starship, and Uncle Luke.' He sends a guilty glance my way when he says the last name.

It turns out that the mystery uncle is Mom's half-brother from Ireland. Uncle Luke is an extreme sports junkie when he is not working for an International Search and Rescue team. On one of his extreme sports activities, he broke his leg, hurt his face, and got scratched up badly. He was too afraid to face Dad and asked Ms Megan to hide him until his broken leg and face healed. Mom was furious when she found out yesterday; it was the longest fifteen minutes of my life. She nearly pulled my ear off. Mom was angry at everyone, me, Uncle Luke, Ms Megan (who was the one that told Mom), and even Adam's father, the absent Advocate, got chewed out. Luckily, Dad saved me. Ms Megan says it is a good thing since the Advocate is staying in Cape Town as a legal advisor to the National Coronavirus Command Council. Now, at least there are two adults in the house with Adam. Mom says calling Uncle Luke an adult is a bit far-fetched. He is a 41-year-old child. When I asked Amelia what Mom meant, she said he behaves like a child doing all those dangerous things like cliff jumping and diving in caves.

An hour later, we have made a list of the spaceships (family) and space colonies (friends) we will report on. We have also divided up the street. Khanyi reports for his house, the gogos' families in KZN and the people on his side of the street. Adam does the neighbours he knows on the north side and I the south. Each of us has seven officers under our command. I can keep Tannie Kotie and Max as officers and Carly as Communications Chief. Adam has added Miss Emmy and the Advocate as officers. Khanyi has settled for his old school friend Jabu from the village and Mr Stegman.

Little did we realise the huge impact our Captain's Log would have in the coming days.

YEAR 3, MONTH 4, WEEK 14

LIFE IN LOCKDOWN

Captain David Zacharias Log

Stardate 73715.41 Log Entry 225

Adam is right; it is like locking in. We are under house arrest. You cannot step outside the gate. I feel sorry for the people living in the flats and apartments; they must stay indoors all the time. If you live in a house, at least you can go and play in the backyard. Mom says a flat with a balcony is now a good investment.

1. *I used to hate the Miller Lockdown Programme, but now I'm glad there is something to do each day. Even the exercising is getting easier, it is more like playing games that make you tired. Amelia has come up with all these fun ideas. We use weights, rubber bands, and tennis balls; she even found an old medicine ball.*
2. *Father Bosinio has sent me an email saying he is volunteering with a church group. He sent some pictures too. Everyone is wearing a mask. I know he is smiling in the pictures though because his eyes crinkle at the corners.*
3. *I texted Jennie. She said they were okay although people have vandalised their shop windows with spray paint. She*

sends me a picture; it reads 'murderers go home'. I WhatsApp her that she is not a murderer. I do not know what else to say.

4. *I pray every day that Adam does not get sick, and that Father Bosinio is safe.*

It takes us a week to set up the daily captains' meetings. On the first Monday, Adam angrily tells us to log off and dress like captains before logging in again. Khanyi and I decide to wear our school blazers as I did not think Mom would like me to wear my church jacket every day. The space station officers didn't need to be told. When they did their first report, they were dressed up in jackets and school blazers. They were taking it so seriously, addressing me as Sir and Captain. When I complained to Max about the whole dress-up thing and everyone being super-serious about this Captain's Log, he told me to get in on the fun. It is cosplay. I've never heard of that before. He then showed me videos of people all over the world acting out Star Trek episodes. Since everyone seems to enjoy the game, I have no choice but to play along.

On Wednesday, Khanyi started to wear a beaded pin with the Star Fleet triangle on a white background. Now everyone wants one. Khanyi emailed us the designs for Captains (red border), Officers (yellow border) and Space Station Commanders (blue border) and Operation Pin Drop got underway. It's the most fun we have had since the lockdown started.

I had not even thought about asking Dad to help us drop off the pins since he's not into playing games, but after Ms Thandeka said no and threatened to lock Khanyi in his room until the twenty-first, I gather my courage to raise the possibility of him helping us with the pin delivery problem. I wait until we have finished lunch – I don't want to spoil the super delicious chicken carbonara with the crispy bacon bits.

'Dad, we made Star Fleet pins for all the officers. Tannie Kotie also helped; she made all the station commander pins. We were wondering if you could help deliver the pins to the officers. Tannie Kotie said she would, but Khanyi said that older people can catch the virus really quick. And Uncle Luke's leg is still broken.' I can see that Dad is listening; he's tapping his finger on his folded left arm and nodding his head but not saying anything. 'Adam said Ms Megan can sterilise everything so there are no germs. We just need to get the pins to Adam's house.'

'What is the plan for collecting the pins?'

'Well, Dad, as the Chief Engineer and Security Officer I was hoping you can help plan and execute Operation Pin Drop.' Dad stands up and walks in the direction of his home office. Mom watches him go. She's smiling.

'Well, you did try.' Amelia starts gathering the plates to take to the kitchen. At the door she bumps into Dad when he returns with pen and paper. Operation Pin Drop is so on!

Chief Security Officer Miller sketches out the plan, sets the times and assigns the tasks. Getting the pins from Officer Kotie is easy – she just drops them in her neighbour's yard with strict handling instructions and they drop them in the next-door neighbour's yard until they reach Starship Zacharias. The problem is crossing the no-go zone to get the pins from Captain Mbulazi. Officers Sullivan and Miller keep watch from the upper deck and radio Chief Miller when the coast is clear, and he teleports to collect the package Captain Mbulazi has dropped out of the cargo hatch. I bet he did not inform First Officer Thandeka of this manoeuvre.

Chief Security Officer Miller uses the ladder extension and delivers all the pins safely into Starship McKenzie's back cargo bay. In a separate black bag are the plastic delivery baggies, each with a name and address.

The next day the bag is returned with military precision by Captain McKenzie with all the sterilised pins neatly addressed to the officers and station commanders.

Officer Stegman's pin is lobbed through the rover window into their cargo hold. There is a bit of a nervous moment when the Community Space Patrol turns into the no-go zone just when the rover is pulling away, but it seems they did not pick up on the delivery.

Chief Miller safely transports provisions and pins to Chief Medical Officer Maximillian Shuler-Brown and Officer Babi.

He makes a detour to Officer Jo with provisions and a pin. After each delivery Chief Miller updates the bridge with a coded message: *'Location 03 cleared.'*

He runs into a bit of trouble when he is stopped on his way out of the safe travel area to Officer Emmy, but the provisions decoy worked out great – and Officer Emmy's grandma waved through the window to the patrol officers. Crisis averted.

Officer Carly goes space walking and waits outside the cargo hold for the Chief. She executes a mid-air intercept and returns safely to the station.

'Location 05 cleared.'

YEAR 3, MONTH 4, WEEK 15

LIFE IN LOCKDOWN – PART 2

Captain David Zacharias Log

STARDATE 73734,71 LOG ENTRY 226

1. *The Miller Lockdown Programme has a new item – Starship Report. At 07:15 every weekday all the reporting officers log in and give their reports. Then I write my report and at 07:45 Captain David Zacharias reports from Starship Zacharias.*
2. *Father Bosinio sometimes sends an email but mostly just a WhatsApp with a picture and a Bible text. I'm happy he is okay and worried that he'll get sick.*
3. *I talk to Jennie once a week. People are still taking out their anger on the shop and have broken two of the windows. Her grandpa is very sad. Jennie says to cheer up her grandpa the family have started to make music again. She sends me a clip of them playing. It sounds strange, different from the music I'm used to hearing.*
4. *Dad says it is okay if I do not remember all the people in my prayers, God knows who I'm praying for. But I always ask God to keep Adam safe just to make sure.*

'Mom, Mom! Dad says the president is going to talk at eight tonight. Do you think he is going to say lockdown is over even though there are still nine days left?'

'No need to yell Davey, I'm right here in the kitchen. Why don't you start on the salad, I've put the ingredients on the table.'

'Beetroot and oranges?'

'Yes – with feta. Use the large side of the grater. And peel the oranges. I'll help you remove the skin from the wedges.'

I eye the small, dark red beetroot, the white bowl is already stained red. 'It will make my hands go red. I'll rather do the feta and oranges. And the pistachios too. I don't wanna do the beet.' Mom slaps down the blue gloves on the table, clearly at the end of her patience. She had a go at Dad earlier when he wanted to use the kitchen table to sort his work papers. She told him that he has his study, her workroom, the den, his workroom outside and he can have the stoep for all she cares, but he must stay out of her kitchen. Not a single piece of paper, tools, or anything else will enter her kitchen, we are all over the house. Enough is enough!

It's as if the house has suddenly become too small for everyone. My room has expanded into the guest room on the first floor while Amelia has taken over the one on the ground floor. Mom was not happy about it but once we promised to clean it ourselves and that everything will be removed by end of lockdown, she reluctantly agreed but kept on threatening to throw everything out if we don't remove the mess by the sixteenth. Now that I have experienced fourteen days of lockdown, I understand why Adam gets so grumpy in his special room. I admire him for staying in a single room for weeks on end. I cannot do it; we even eat lunch outside just to get out of the house.

'Don't worry, I'll do it. You peel the oranges.' Amelia, in a frilly pink apron, puts on the blue gloves and starts on the grisly task of grating beets. Today she's wearing a long red skirt with tiny white flowers and a white sweater top with black ribbing, her blond hair is pulled in messy bun. I look down, and see she is wearing white sneakers – she'd better be careful with the beet. Even Mom has been dressing up all through lockdown. Today she is wearing a khaki green shirt dress with dark grey leggings and a long sleeveless cardigan in a darker green than the dress. I catch sight of my reflection in the fridge door, a chubby boy dressed in sloppy grey sweatpants and dark blue hoodie. I cannot even remember brushing my hair today. Amelia notices me staring and makes big eyes at me.

'You should start dressing properly. It will make you feel better. Carly says the president is going to extend the lockdown.' For a moment she is silent. The she bangs the grater on the plate and throws the beet back into the bowl. The red juices spatter everywhere. 'This is so unfair. I'm missing out on my last year at school. I've worked so hard to get onto the swim team and we did not even have one meet. This isn't right. What if they cancel the matric dance? I've already decided on my dress.'

'Amelia, you are overreacting. I'm sure everything will normalise in a few months.'

'Mom, they don't even have a vaccine yet. Max says it will be months before there is one. In the meantime, we are stuck in here and life is passing us by.'

'Well, it is still months to go before your matric farewell and Mr De Wet says we are living in historic times. You can tell your grandchildren that you lived through COVID.'

'Gmmf, you are just happy that you don't have to go to school.'

'High school isn't so bad.' A deathly silence follows my words. When I look up, both women are staring at me. 'I have Max and Legs. They are my friends, so it's okay.' They keep looking at me, the silence stretching. 'Mom, I think the meat is burning,' Smoke is curling from the pan on the stove.

'Oh no!' Mom quickly removes the pan and dumps the now

very blackish chicken strips on the plate. 'Look what you made me do.'

'I didn't do anything! I was just saying that school is okay. It is you who keeps staring at me. Amelia is just mad because she cannot see Sir Rocco.'

'That's not true!'

'I've seen the two of you talking and laughing, while you are supposed to be practising. He even gave you a lift after school.'

'Amelia. Who is this boy and since when does he have a driver's licence?' Amelia gives me a death-ray glare and I wisely keep my head down peeling oranges while Amelia starts to explain.

At eight that evening, President Cyril Ramaphosa asks his fellow South Africans to endure even longer. To make sacrifices so that our country may survive the Coronavirus crisis and save tens of thousands of lives. The Level 5 nationwide lockdown is to be extended by a further two weeks until the end of April. Most of the existing lockdown measures will remain in force including the ban on cigarettes and alcohol which seems to be a very big deal for some people.

On Good Friday, the Coronavirus hits close to home, and it's Adam who reports the first case in our galaxy.

Captain's log Starship McKenzie

STARDATE 10 APRIL 2020 ENTRY 3-023

Captain Adam Sullivan McKenzie's Coronavirus Report
All personnel on the McKenzie Starship are healthy. Officer Luke's leg is still healing.
Senior Legal Officer Ian at Cape Town Space Station says he is healthy. He has nothing to report.
Space Station Chief Jo says he is keeping an eye on everyone. All

personnel are healthy and eating well. They will have to start exercising soon else their uniforms will not fit. They are getting fat.

Adam stops reading and looks at his mom over his shoulder. Ms Megan gives a quick nod and Adam starts reading again.

Education Officer Emily on Space Station Bumblebee reported the first case of Coronavirus on the station. Ensign Wentworth's mother has been taken to the hospital during the night. She is in ICU. Ms Wentworth's status is critical. We must pray for her and her family.

End of Report

When Adam finishes reading his report, we all sit in silence – our game has suddenly become very real. Ms Megan touches him on the back. 'I'm proud of you. You gave a good report.'

I remember my role. 'Thank you, Captain McKenzie. Please keep us informed.' The knot in my stomach twists tighter. The familiar routine keeps me from freaking out. 'Captain Mbulazi, please give your report.' Over his shoulder I can see Grandma Simi putting a handkerchief to her mouth and reaching out to the person sitting next to her. I listen to Captain Mbulazi reading his report, but today the words make no sense. My mind is caught in an endless loop, only hearing that Ms Wentworth is ill, she is in ICU. *Please don't die. Please don't die.*

Later that day Ms Megan asks that the officers rather do their own reports, it would lessen the stress on Adam when reporting about people getting sick and dying. All the officers are excited to report live. Dad creates a meeting link that he sends to everyone. Since there are no time differences, Grandpa Heinz logs in from Hanover. The first few broadcasts you can see Grandma Edith's thin-lipped disapproval, but it does not take long before she quite happily stays logged in to chat to

Tannie Kotie and the gogos after the Starship Report. The Advocate never logs in – he has no time for such frivolous games.

When Khanyi logs in the next day, we can see Gogo Simi and Gogo Nonhla, dressed in black, sitting in the background, Ms Thandeka with Remo standing next to her and Keeya wearing her school blazer. After the customary greeting Khanyi starts his report and sets the tone for all future meetings.

Captain's log Starship Lebombo

STARDATE 11 APRIL 2020 ENTRY 3-024

Captain Khanyi Mpilo Mbulazi reporting. Present today is First Officer Simi, Officer Nonhla, Chief Operations Officer Thandeka, and Enlisted Personnel Keeya and Remothabhile.

Remo waves her hand in the background. 'My name is Remo, not the other name. I'm Remo. You must say that.' Khanyi gives her a dirty look, takes a deep breath and continues with the report. Gogo Nonhla touches her shoulder and shakes her head. Remo reluctantly stops protesting. Khanyi is going to get it later.

Station Commander Jabu reports that Retired Medical Officer Thandanani Mpilo Patrick Ndawo has passed away this morning at six twenty due to COVID-19 related complications. He was 73 years old and worked as a doctor for 42 years. He is the second son of Dumisani Solomon Ndawo. Brother to Gogo Nonhla and Simi. He was married to Thabisa and has three sons and one daughter. We ask for a minute of silence for the one who has passed.

I watch the seconds slip by; there is nothing in my head. Khanyi resumes his report, listing the sick, the ones in hospital and the ones who have died. He reads each person's name and their age. Gogo Simi uses a little black handkerchief to wipe her tears. It reminds me of Father Bosinio and his big black handkerchief that he tied around my head the day we first met. I hope he is okay.

Mom has switched the radio to music while she and Amelia do the dishes. She says an update once a day is enough. But I must know, and I go looking for Dad. He's in the den, watching the news. When I walk in, the screen flashes the latest statistic for South Africa. On Saturday, 11 April 2020, the total number of cases in South Africa is 2 028 and the total number of deaths, 25. The latest person to die is a 61-year-old man from the Western Cape. His underlying medical conditions included diabetes, hypertension, and obesity. I want to ask Dad what type of illness hypertension is. I'm sure Adam will know; he knows lots of medical words. The reporter starts reading the worldwide figures and for one shameful moment I'm proud that South Africa is doing better than Europe and America. The WHO has recorded 1 248 335 infections worldwide and the death toll is at 118 684 and rising. Today 6 616 people have died. For the second day in a row over nine hundred people have died in America. America... Italy… Germany... I feel more and more anxious as the countries and rising numbers scroll by.

A WHO official comes on the screen. He looks tired, like Dad after a long day with back-to-back meetings. He is talking to an off-screen reporter. *Since the hospitals are coping better and with enforced restrictions the recovery rate is at 81,86%.*

'Dad, does that mean you have an 81% chance to get well again? That's good, is it not? You are not going to die if you get sick?'

'Yes David, but let's not rush it, we do not know how accurate the figures are. We still do not have a vaccine and twenty out of a hundred people are still dying. It also depends on the country – Italy and the UK have a much lower recovery rate because they have a lot of very old citizens who are not able to recover. More countries have now started to enforce some type of lockdown. But when lockdown is lifted, it might create a spike in infections again.' Dad gives me a smile. 'But it looks like the human race is fighting back again, Captain Zacharias. Now we only need a vaccine.'

'Chief Medical Officer Maximillian Shuler-Brown and his team is on it. We just need to hang in there, Chief Miller.'

YEAR 3, MONTH 4, WEEK 16

CABIN FEVER

Captain David Zacharias Log

STARDATE 73773,31 LOG ENTRY 227

1. *Wake up at 06:30*
2. *Captain's meeting at 07:45.*
3. *Breakfast at 08:30*
4. *School homework from 09:00 until 11:00*
5. *Break and cleaning of my room, bathroom and guestroom.*
6. *12:30: help Mom with lunch when it is my turn.*
7. *13:00 to 14:00: lunch.*
8. *14:00: rake leaves in yard and sweep the stoep.*
9. *15:00 to 16:30: play time.*
10. *16:45 to 17:30: Energiser Bunny gym activities, except Thursdays and Sundays.*
11. *18:00: help Mom with dinner when it is my turn.*
12. *19:00 to 20:00: dinner and cleaning up.*
13. *20:00 to 21:30: Me time*
14. *21:30 to 22:00: Getting ready for bed.*
15. *22:00: lights out.*

Over and over and over again. How am I going to do this for fourteen more days…

Dad says we have cabin fever. More like house fever. He says when you are confined indoors for an extended period of time you start to feel restless, bored, irritable, snappy, and moody. These are all signs of cabin fever. It is good to have a routine, eat regularly, keep active and communicate with friends and family daily. When Mom starts to tap her fingers on the table Dad had to explain quickly. He tells us that we need to keep our brains active with new things. It is time to challenge ourselves … and then he drops his cure for cabin fever on the table: 'We are going to build a mezzanine floor.'

'Hank, you are being ridiculous. How are the four of us going to build a floor. Up in the air. The kids are going to get hurt.'

Dad calmly continues to roll open the drawing on the table. He puts the salt and pepper shakers on the corners to keep the plan from rolling back. He lifts Mom's hand, gives the back a kiss and puts her hand down to keep the bottom corner in place. I put my hand on the other corner. 'Dad, what is a mezzanine floor?'

'We are going to build a mezzanine floor from tomorrow.'

'What is that?' Adam is leaning into the camera as if he can see the floor.

'Ugh, sit back, I don't want to see your nose boogers. Eeewww, it's gross, get out of the camera! It is a special floor. Dad says is a like half a floor, it does not go from wall to wall. It is like building a balcony inside a room.'

'Why do you want to do that? Where are you going to build the balcony?' Khanyi is not impressed by the idea. He does not even look up from the magazine he's reading.

'It's not a balcony, it's a floor. We are going to build it in the garage. Dad has plans and everything.'

'Your dad is an engineer; he cannot build a floor. You must be a builder. Your balcony is going to fall.'

'Is not. My dad can build anything. He learned to build things in the army.' I keep quiet about the fact that Mom seems to be of the same opinion as Khanyi. I don't know if it is because she doesn't trust Dad or his helpers.

'I'm building things too.' Adam pipes up. 'We have plans and instructions.'

'No, you're not,' says Khanyi. 'You are just saying that.'

'I'm not. Why are you so horrid? You're just jealous. I'm building a ship with Uncle Luke. It is a battleship. It's called… I can't remember the name. But it's for aircraft.'

'You're a big fat liar and I'm not talking to you.' The next moment Khanyi has logged off.

Adam is in tears. 'I'm not lying. I'm building too. Khanyi is so mean.'

'It's okay, Adam. I believe you. I think Khanyi has cabin fever. It must be worse for him. He is the only boy in the house.'

'Cabin fever? It that a new pandemic like Corona? Is he going to die? I don't want him to die. I'm not mad at him anymore. Is there medicine for cabin fever? Why are you laughing? Khanyi is sick.'

'Not sick-sick. It's because he must stay in the house all the time, so he is irritable, snappy, and moody. He needs a change. Dad says we must challenge our brain by doing something new. Like building stuff.'

'Like me. I've never ever built a model ship before. It's so large, we are building it in the poolroom, I wish you could see it.' Adam's eyes lose their sparkle, and he looks sad again.

'Why don't you send me pictures of your ship and I'll send you a picture of the floor.'

'Okay.' Adam pulls at his too-long hair. He is seriously in need of a haircut. 'Is Khanyi going to be okay? He can borrow my puzzles. That's like building too. Then he will not be sick anymore. Will you ask him. He is mad at me.'

'I'll text him. He's offline. Remember to send me a picture before you go to bed.'

Khanyi is ignoring all my messages. Even after I told him about the model ship building kit Mom gave to Uncle Luke for Christmas. It is a model of the aircraft carrier USS Kitty Hawk. He also did not answer when I told him that Adam is not mad at him anymore and he can borrow his puzzles.

The next day at two we line up outside the garage. I'm dressed as per instructions in old denims and a fitted tee. Dad said no sloppy tops. We must also wear closed shoes. I'm wearing an old faded pair of red All Stars. Dad hands out the personal protection equipment, PPE for short. A white hard hat with our names on it, but Mom's hat says Boss Lady. And gloves that fit properly, Dad must have been planning this for a while. I snap a selfie of us all dressed up and send it to Khanyi and Adam.

'Today we are only setting up – we are not building yet. The first task is to move all the stuff out of the construction footprint. We are going to stack everything neatly on the left side of the garage. Then we are going to bring in the scaffolding. Davey and I will move the heavy stuff. Let's get started.' Two hours later I'm all sweating, dusty and tired but all the boxes, two carpets and tools are neatly stacked on the left side.

'Okay. All done, let's bring in the scaffolding.'

'Hank, slow down. I'm thirsty – we all need a break. Amelia, help me to get the drinks. You two, go wash your hands. Use the garden tap.' Mom pulls off her hat and wipes at the sweat with the dark blue cloth around her neck. 'I've never been so dirty in my life.'

After a quick drink we are at it again. This time we carry the steel frames; they may look light, but it needs two of us. Amelia and I pair up for this task. Then the braces and tie bars. When it's time for assembling the scaffolding, the mystery of the steel rings in the ceiling and walls is finally solved. It's to hook up the block-and-tackle pulley system. I can't wait to show Adam the clip. He'll be so surprised. With the pulley, one person can easily lift the frame while the others lock it into place. It doesn't take too long before the two towers are up and wheeled into position, and then we lift and lock the bridge in place.

'We're done, that's it for today. We can start the building tomorrow.'

'Dad? Dad, can I go up there? Please.'

'I want to go too.' Amelia bats her baby blues at Dad.

'No, it's dangerous,' says Mom, putting a stop to our adventure.

'Bubbles, dear. They are going to work up there. Let them roll out the rubber mat. I'll watch them.'

Mom gives a big sigh. 'Please be careful, we cannot take you to hospital.'

'Yes, Mom,' we chorus. And dash for opposite towers.

'Slowly!'

I climb carefully and slowly up the ladder to the bridge. I'm glad for the railing as it looks quite high from up here. 'Dad, how high is this?'

'The bridge is at 2,8 metres. Watch out for the matting.' The pulley easily lifts the mat and I pull it closer with Amelia's help. 'Start on the one end and roll it out. It will keep us from slipping on the metal surface.'

I give Amelia a high five before we climb down slowly under Mom's watchful eyes. 'I'm hungry. What's for dinner?'

'Get cleaned up first. It's Asian fishcakes ala Jamie Oliver for dinner. This time I'm adding the ginger and chilli. Don't know what viruses we picked up in that dirty garage.'

'Hey, that is a clean garage…'

That evening, I fell asleep thinking that today was a good day. We had fun today, Mom was smiling and looked more relaxed at dinner. She even surprised us with yoghurt ice cream for dessert. I'm glad that Khanyi has stopped sulking and asked if he could borrow the puzzles. I watch from the window when he slips out the gate to collect them. Adam calls hello from the stoep and Khanyi tells him to stay safe. All is well in the neighbourhood.

The next morning the dying starts.

STARDATE 16 APRIL 2020 ENTRY 3-029

I listen to Horticulture Officer, Kotie Klopper, reporting for Starship Zacharias. She reads the three names slowly, pausing after each name.

Aletta Johanna de Beer, 63, Marthinus Phillipus Gabriel de Beer, 77. Jakobus Benjamin Vermaak 48. Aletta and Phillip were married for 43 years. Their son, Phil and daughter Caylee live in the UK. They have four grandchildren. Phillip loved to grow all kinds of pumpkins. Aletta liked cooking and baking –so it was a good match.

Ben never married. He did not talk much. He would instead draw funny comic strips. He once drew one in church and showed it to Deacon Samuel. The Deacon was laughing so much he had to leave but he forgot the windows were open and we could hear him laughing outside. Ben and his comics will be missed.

We ask for a minute of silence for the ones that have passed away.

That evening at dinner, the landline rings. Dad goes to answer the call. We all stop eating, straining to hear the conversation. After a while he comes in. He takes his seat quietly but does not start eating again.

'Hank. Is everything okay? What was the phone call about?'

Dad wipes his hand over his face. Perhaps he did not hear Mom's question. He lines up his knife and fork, takes Mom's hand before speaking. 'That was the son of Mr and Mrs De Beer that passed away. He called to say thank you. He says thank you to Davey, Adam and Khanyi for remembering his parents. They passed away at the old age home, he could not be there for them. He cannot attend their funeral because he is living in the UK. Tannie Kotie has sent him the link for the Starship report. He... he says thank you...' Dad's voice breaks. Then he gets up and leaves the room.

Mom pushes her chair back. 'Finish dinner and clear the table.' She follows Dad.

Amelia and I look at each other. I'm suddenly not hungry anymore. 'Finish your food, Davey. You know Mom will stress if we are not eating.'

I help Amelia clear the table. And wash the dishes. I take my time folding and hanging up the blue and red checked drying cloths. 'Amelia why did Mr De Beer call to say thank you. We didn't do anything. We're just playing... it's a school project. I do not understand.'

Amelia stops wiping the already-dry sink. I watch how she carefully wrings out the cloth to avoid water droplets on the shiny silver surface. 'I think it's about closure and being remembered. Mom says that funerals are to say goodbye and to talk about that person's life. There are no real funerals now. It's rushed and people are scared to attend. They die all alone in hospitals and you cannot say goodbye. That is what the Starship Report does, it gives the people who stay behind closure.' She hangs up the cloth smoothing it out. 'Did you know that Ms Megan asked Adam if he wants to stop doing the Starship Report and that he said no.'

'I didn't know that.'

'Adam told Ms Megan that he cannot stop, it is important to tell God that the people who died are loved ones and he must take care of them specially. He is writing down all the names in a memory book. He said that the Advocate always says to do a good and right thing is hard, while a wrong thing is easy. He knows it's hard, but he wants to do the Starship Report.'

The next moment Amelia gives me a big hug. 'I'm proud of you little brother. I'm happy to be part of this journey with you.'

I didn't know that I needed this hug. I put my arms around her slim body and squeeze her right back. Then I get embarrassed and push her away. 'Do you think Dad is okay?'

'Yes. He just doesn't deal well with mushy stuff. I'm sure he's proud of you.'

I look away, saying the first thing that comes to mind. 'Should we make tea for them.' I can hear Amelia laugh while she fills the kettle. I pretend not to hear, but I cannot help but smile while taking the yellow polka dot mugs from the cupboard. Dad really does not do mushy stuff, as soon as Amelia starts crying or gets emotional, he flees the room. If it's Mom, he just keeps hugging her.

On Friday Education Officer Emily on Space Station Bumblebee logs in and shortly after, Big H followed by the Crunch with his arms around his mother and sister. He looks even bigger and more serious than usual. We wait, but Wentworth never logs in.

STARDATE 17 APRIL 2020 ENTRY 3-030

Education Officer Emily reporting from Space Station Bumblebee. Ms Susanna Wentworth passed away late last night. She was 43 years old. She leaves behind her husband, Carl, son Peter and daughter Sonia. Ms Wentworth was my Grade 2 teacher; she was always singing in class. I'll always remember Ms Wentworth as an amazing teacher that had the ability to make kids love school and learning. We ask for a minute of silence for her.

We didn't work on the mezzanine on Friday either. Dad's busy with urgent work, and we only see him at lunch and dinner. Mom threatened to call his boss if he does not take time off. After that, he started showing up for gym class. We go through the motions, but everyone is quiet, busy with their own thoughts. I'm glad to escape to my room after dinner and the company of Adam, Khanyi, Legs and Max. That evening, I crept into Amelia's room and lay down at the bottom end. She kind of woke and started to pat my feet, which made me laugh. She kicked me in the stomach and threatened to throw me out.

YEAR 3, MONTH 4, WEEK 17

WHEN WILL CORONA BE DONE?

Captain David Zacharias Log

STARDATE 73792,62 LOG ENTRY 228

1. *Amelia says the Black Death Plague lasted four years, so did the Russian flu of the late 1800s but the Spanish flu of 1918 only a year. All pandemics after that usually lasted one to two years.*
    1. *Max says it's because science in the modern era has evolved to fight viruses quickly.*
    2. *Yoda (the pain in the butt), says the Coronavirus will be done when it's done, we cannot force it.*

I am tired. I don't sleep well. I wake up early in the mornings while it's still dark. I'm too restless to stay in bed. I stand at the window and imagine other people asleep. Sometimes it feels as if my breath is stuck inside, and I open the window and let the cold morning air in. I don't mind the cold. It makes me feel alive. I wait for the sun to come up before I get back in bed and pretend to sleep. I wonder what the Sky House looks like in the autumn sun. When Mom worries about my room being cold, I tell her winter is coming.

Captain's log Starship Zacharias

STARDATE 21 APRIL 2020 ENTRY 3-034

This is Day 26 since Starfleet Commander-In-Chief Cyril Ramaphosa ordered a Level 5 Lockdown.
Captain David Miller reports all personnel are in good health and are keeping busy with various activities.
Senior Officer Bosinio at Space Station Italy reports that he is healthy, and we should have faith.

Starfleet released the World Health Organisation report for 21 April 2020.
Total number of cases 1 730 947 with 999 158 recoveries reported. Total world deaths 189 458
For the same date South Africa has 3 465 reported cases with 1199 in Gauteng. The recoveries are 1 055 that is a 30,45% recovery rate. Number of deaths is 58.
Horticulture Officer Kotie Klopper to present the report for her section.
End of Captain's Report

This must be what prisoners feel when they are getting out of jail. On Thursday evening the 23rd of April 2020, exactly seven weeks since lockdown started, President Cyril Ramaphosa informed his fellow South Africans that '*our people need to eat. They need to earn a living. Companies need to be able to produce and to trade, they need to generate revenue and keep their employees in employment.*' Then he said the words that I did not understand but made everyone sigh with relief… '*beyond Thursday, 30 April, we should begin a gradual and phased recovery of economic activity.*'

'Dad, what does that mean?'

'It means that from the first of May we are moving from Level 5 to Level 4. Selected businesses in specific economic sectors will be allowed to open with a work-from-home strategy. I guess it will be essential services only. Still no travelling and borders will remain closed. Only essential travelling is allowed.

We will have to wait until the Health Minister gives more details.'

'And school, Dad?'

'Sorry Davey, no school yet. But it will be soon now. We better get that floor done. We will start tomorrow at eleven, break for lunch at one and start again at two.'

'Slow down Hank, we don't need to build the floor in one day. Let's pace ourselves with putting the steel beams in tomorrow and the floor on Saturday.' Mom starts gathering the cups. 'Come on you two, get ready for bed, it's late. You heard Dad; tomorrow is a full day.'

'It seems like school is never going to start again. The president did not even give a hint.' Amelia shares my feelings about going back to school, but I think she's more impatient than me.

'Maybe the Minister will say something. But the Grade 12s are attending virtual classes, so you are already back at school.'

'It's not the same. You don't understand. You cannot just talk to people and… and it's strange. I want to sit in a classroom, hear the noise, the bell, everything. I just miss everything about school. What about you?'

'I just miss getting out of the house. It will be nice to see Max and Legs again. In person. I want to go to music lessons with Adam.' I follow her up the stairs, passing the pictures on the wall. 'Do you think I should play rugby again?'

'Did you like playing rugby?' We both look at the group picture of my first big rugby game. It seems so long ago. I remember being happy when the photo was taken; I'm smiling in the picture even with Big H's arm around my neck.'

'Sometimes it was fun. Like that day. Other days were hard. I'm stronger and fitter now.'

'Seems like your mind is half made up. You still have time to think it over.' Then she sprints up the stairs. 'I'm calling dibs on the bathroom!'

'Hey, it's my turn to be first. Amelia, you are cheating, it's my turn.' The door slamming shut is my only answer. And as always, I wish I had my own bathroom like Khanyi.

We are in for a surprise the next day. Mom is in charge of construction. Now I know why her hard hat says *Boss Lady*. Turns out Khanyi was right (I'm never telling him that), Dad is good with design, but Mom knows construction. She helped Granddad Sully build the sheds, workshop and cottages on the farm. Mom and Dad met in the hardware stored owned by Granddad Sully. He went to the store to complain about the quantity of building sand delivered and ran into Mom. She was wearing a short pink sundress with heeled sandals. He cannot remember the colour of the sandals; he was floored by her legs. Whenever Dad says that Mom smiles and asks if he is a 'legs' man now, and Dad blushes bright red. I think I'm more of a 'hair' man. I first noticed Jennie's long, brown hair that looks like melted chocolate and only then her eyes.

By one o'clock, only three of the six steel beams are in place and while I look and smell like I've done construction, Amelia looks like a model from one of those outdoor advertisements in faded black denims and a red checked shirt. The only sign that she is working hard is the rolled-up sleeves. Mom's wearing paint-spattered fitted denims with a dark blue tee under a man's shirt. Dad is looking all professional in his blue coveralls with his name on the back. I once again realise how sloppily I dress, glancing down at my stretched grey tee now covered in sweat.

After a delicious workman's lunch of toasted English muffins, tomato salsa and a fried egg, all made on the gas braai, we finish putting up the last three steel beams and stop for the day. I don't know what hurts the most, my shoulders or my legs. I've done more squats today than all the Energiser Bunny gym days put together.

Amelia is also favouring the back of her shoulder. 'Mom, could you please put ointment on my back. It hurts. I'm glad we are done with beams they are really heavy.' While Mom and Amelia are chatting, I slip away, today I'm calling dibs on the bathroom.

YEAR 3, MONTH 5, WEEK 18

FREEDOM DAY

Captain David Zacharias Log

STARDATE 73811,91 LOG ENTRY 229

1. *This is the week that locking in is done. We are finally going to leave through the gate!*
2. *I'll be able to ride my bike, Firefly, outside the yard.*
3. *I'll see Adam and Khanyi in the flesh.*

Although South Africa's official Freedom Day falls on 27 April, I'm sure more people secretly celebrated the 1st of May as Freedom Day. By six I'm ready and waiting at the front door. 'C'mon people, time for exercise is running out. We must be back inside at nine.' I've been counting the hours and minutes since the announcement was made on Wednesday, 29 of April. I can't wait to ask Khanyi if he really ordered pizza for breakfast, since the regulations now allow people to order in food. Amelia was way more excited about the fact that she can now buy cosmetics again. She already talked Dad into taking her along to the shops. Although the gyms will also be open, Dad vetoed that with a single NO. I don't care, I'm simply happy to be outside.

When I finally push my bike though the gate it feels as if I can breathe again. Ms Megan, Uncle Luke and Adam, wearing an oxygen mask connected to a bottle in a special backpack, are already waiting outside. Across the road Khanyi waves hello, one of the gogos has Remo by the hand. It is cool, about 10 degrees Celsius, and the sun isn't up properly. Mindful of the social distancing commandments issued by the parents and the warning that this privilege can disappear if we dare to mess up, the three of us set off. It's so quiet; no cars, no people. We wave to Officer Stegman waiting on his stoep for the troops to gather. We pass Horticultural Officer Kotie on her way back, her trolley already emptied of fresh fruit and vegetables.

'Good morning, Captains. You are out early.'

'Morning Chief! It's the first day of freedom. No time to waste.'

We circle the block, catching up with parents, passing them and go around the block again. My mask is hot, and it is difficult to breathe when we go fast. 'Hey slow down. I need to catch my breath. Adam, are you okay? I'm glad your mom said you can go biking.'

'Not Mommy. Uncle Luke. He said I can use the oxygen mask with the cloth mask as insurance. Did you eat pizza for breakfast? I wanted to but Mommy said no. Did you?'

'No. Gogo Simi said that is not proper food. We must eat mealie pap to stay strong. Gogo Nonhla is making breakfast, she promised to make scrambled eggs with the pap.'

'That's kind of strange. Like something Adam's Aunt Mabel would cook up.'

'Gogo Nonhla is like Aunt Mabel.' Adam's voice is muffled but we can hear him giggle. 'It's going to taste horrible.'

'It tastes GOOD. I'm sure you would like it. The salty eggs and the mealie pap just go together. You should try. You should ask your mom to make it.'

'I don't think Mommy knows how to make mealie pap.'

'Uncle Luke can make mealie pap. You can ask him.'

'Hey kids, last round. It's past seven already and I'm hungry. You can hear my stomach growl from the next street. Make it quick or I'll die of hunger.'

'But it's still early, we can stay out until nine.'

Uncle Luke shakes his head. 'No, kiddo. The oxygen does not last that long. You can go biking again tomorrow. Let's not stress out the moms.'

We take the last trip around the block real slow.

Stardate 01 May 2020 Entry 3-044

CHIEF TREASURY OFFICER STEGMAN REPORTING FOR STARSHIP LEBOMBO

We have received news that my mother-in-law has taken ill. Officer Stegman is checking to see if she can visit, since the illness appears to be non-COVID-related. The balance of the department is in good health and have enjoyed the early morning exercise.

Father Tilly confirmed that a church service will be held for Ms Mary on Tuesday. Only 50 people will be allowed; kindly book with the church office.

On Saturday afternoon, we finish laying the last of the floor beams. Even though I'm tired and dirty it feels great to see the end result of all our hard work. We take selfies lying on the newly installed floor and sitting on the edge, our legs dangling in space.

'There are no stairs, how are we going to get up and down? Are we going to put up a ladder like in a tree house?' Dad calls me over and starts knocking on the wall. At first everything sounds the same and then there is a hollow sound. 'There's a door in the wall?'

'Not a door yet, just the opening, covered by wood and plastered over. We'll start putting up the stairs next week. First, we must move the scaffolding outside.'

'Wow, Dad you thought of everything.'

'See the grooves over there. That's where we are going to fit the walls in. It's for a small bathroom; the plumbing is already installed behind a panel; we just need to open it up and connect.'

Excited, I start knocking on the wall until I find the wood panel. I didn't know it was up here. I can't wait to tell the others; they will be so surprised by the hidden door and room. It's really a garage house like Adam calls our double storey four vehicle garage.

We never got around to building the stairs the next week. Nor the week thereafter. I had to wait a long time for the hidden door to be revealed.

YEAR 3, MONTH 5, WEEK 19

Captain David Zacharias Log

STARDATE 73831,21 LOG ENTRY 230

On Sunday, 4 May 2020, at 14:23 South African time, Father Umberto Bosinio dies of COVID-19 related complications. He was 55 years old.

I wake suddenly, already in motion. I'm cold and my neck hurts from sleeping in the chair. For a brief moment I'm confused by my surroundings and the reason for sleeping in the den. Then it all comes back. Warm tears burn my eyes, I close them quickly, keeping them inside. I want to go to sleep but my mind doesn't let me. He's dead. Father Bosinio is dead. He died yesterday. I'm crying again. Quietly, not the huge, ugly screaming crying of yesterday, I'm just… crying.

'Davey, I've made you green tea with honey. You must get ready, it's after seven and the Starship Report is starting soon.'

I glare at Amelia. 'I'm not going to. Go away. I don't want

your tea.' I push pass her and run up the stairs. I get into bed and pull the blanket over my head. My breathing sounds loud in my ears. Father Bosinio doesn't breathe anymore; he is dead.

'David. Sit up. Adam is on the phone for you.' I want to shout at Dad to leave, but I cannot. I remember Dad hugging me close while I was screaming and crying last night. He didn't leave. He stayed with me. The light is hurting my eyes. I take the phone from Dad. It's a video call.

The moment Adam sees my face he starts talking. 'You must do the Starship Report. You have to, Father Bosinio expects it from you. Do it properly. He's our friend; we have to honour him...' Adam starts to cry.

'This is stupid – a game. It changes nothing. I don't want to do it anymore. Leave me alone. You can do it yourself. Leave me out of it.'

'It is your report. You started it. How can you give up? It is for Father Bosinio. He's our friend.'

'I can do what I want. You are his friend too – you can do the report. I don't care about this silly game...'

'STOP!' Khanyi's shout shocks us into silence. It's so out of character for Yoda to yell. 'It's not silly. It's not a game. It's real. People are dying alone. No one wants to go to funerals; the dead are forgotten. Gogo Nonhla says what we are doing is good. We are holding a light for them. I'm making an album and Adam is writing their names in a book so that they are remembered.' A wrinkled old face appears over Khanyi's shoulder, kind brown eyes catch and hold mine.

'*Ingane,* you have a good heart. This work that you are doing brings peace. It makes my heart ache a little bit less. When I go, you must put me on this TV box and say goodbye. You must say my name, uGogo Nonhla, Thandeka Ndawo...'

'Gogo, no!' Khanyi puts his arms around her neck. 'Don't say stuff like that. You are going to live for a long time.'

'*Thula, thula*. It's life. Go. Go, say the words for this man who has passed through your life. It is right.'

Captain's log Starship Zacharias

STARDATE 05 MAY 2020 ENTRY 3-048

Captain David Miller reporting for Starship Zacharias.
Level 4 COVID-19 lockdown regulations are being followed.
The following personnel are present at the meeting. Captains, announce yourselves.

My voice sounds strange to my ears. Hoarse and off-key.

Captain Adam Sullivan McKenzie of the Starship McKenzie – all personnel present and accounted for.
Captain Khanyi Mpilo Mbulazi of the Starship Lebombo – all personnel present and accounted for.
Education Officer Emily reporting for Space Station Bumblebee – all personnel present and accounted for.

One by one, the officers state their names. Today I'm glad for our strange greeting ritual Adam insisted upon and Khanyi, who usually does the opposite of what Adam wants, agreed with. Today it gives me time to order my thoughts. I forgot to write in Grandma Edith's journal last night. I must remember to do that today. Dad has given me a copy of the funeral letter that Father Tilly emailed early this morning. They must have known he was sick. When I hear Grandfather's voice, I know my time is up, for he is the last to report in. I click on the gallery and the screen fills up with the seventeen small windows into peoples' lives. I can see Father Tilly at his desk wearing his church robes. On the left of the screen the three priests who worked with Father Bosinio are huddled together, the white of their collars glowing in the low light, their faces covered with black masks. Max and his Babi are sitting in the kitchen, I can see the flower plate on the wall. I find Adam in the third row, second from the right. He sees me looking and nods his head.

On Sunday, 4 May 2020, our friend, Father Umberto Francesco Bosinio passed away from COVID-19-related complications. He was 55 years old. Adam and I met Father Bosinio two years ago. It rained that day. He was sad because there was no thunder. He liked our highveld storms with the thunder and lighting. Father Bosinio used to say that God is showing off his superpowers. He was a big man with a big voice. He was my friend and I will miss him very much. He always told us to have faith.

I have faith that we'll meet again.

Today we stand for a minute of silence for Father Bosinio, our friend who has died.

I do not close my eyes, instead I study the picture that I have put on the screen. It was taken on the day of the St Michael's race. The big man has his arms spread wide, his robes covered by a black T-shirt announcing him as team leader, and, as always, he is laughing. For a moment I can hear his laughter, his voice telling me to have faith. Tears blur his picture.

End of Captain's Report.

YEAR 3, MONTH 5, WEEK 20

COVID IS STILL WITH US

Captain David Zacharias Log

STARDATE 73850,51 LOG ENTRY 231

1. *Jennie's grandpa died in his sleep, and she asked me to read out his name in the Starship Report. She had to teach me how to say his name. First his surname and then his names, Chen Jie Qiang.*
2. *Carly's Dad-Dad is sick. His son is looking after him at home. When Carly does her report, she talks so fast that I only understand the report after she stops talking.*
3. *I get up at six to go biking. It's the best part of my day. One day I'm going to stay outside until nine.*
4. *Uncle Luke has taken off his cast by himself. He says that the doctors are too busy. Adam has sent us the video of him sawing through the cast. Khanyi complains that his family is boring, nothing exciting happens in their house.*
5. *The Maths and Science teachers have set up online classes. Max and I are doing homework together.*
6. *Ms Roux is also giving music lessons online. We now have an orchestra class once a week. In the beginning, it was chaos, but the twelve of us are getting our act together, and*

when Ms Roux gives the signal, we start playing at the same time. Sort of…

On Wednesday, I received a video message from Father Bosinio. I do not want to watch it; I'm angry at him that that he did not stay safe and died, but I'm also sad at the same time. When I told Mom about the video she asked if she could watch it with me. At first, I wanted to watch it alone, but I was too scared. I waited until the evening, and we watched it together in the den.

He was already sick when he made the video. At times he had to stop, and the nurse would help him to put the oxygen mask back on. I thought he would be sad to die, but he said he was excited to go home to God. He had a good life and he had made friends all over the world. He told me it's okay to be sad, but only for a short time. He said we must remember him with happiness. He will watch over us. He says that he has faith that I'll grow up strong with a good heart.

Afterwards we just sit, lost in our memories, sipping hot Milo. After a while, Amelia leans over and whispers to Mom, 'I find his Italian accent very sexy.'

'Mmm, quite sultry and that voice.'

Dad starts coughing, his Milo going down the wrong way. Mom pats him on the back. 'You okay, hon?'

He looks at the two women in our family. I share his shock and confusion. Amelia starts to giggle, Mom's dimples put in an appearance.

'He was a priest, but also a man.'

'*Ragazzo*,' mimics Amelia.

'Bubbles?!'

'*Signora* Bubbles,' goes Amelia, echoing Dad.

Nervously, I start laughing, Dad looks so confused, his brows wrinkled up, his eyes jumping from Amelia to Mom, who is keeping an innocent face.

Dad tries again, 'Bubbles?'

'*Sì*?' Mom is sitting up straight, her hands neatly folded in her lap.

'This is not the appropriate time.'

'Yes, dear…'

I flee the room, followed by a laughing Amelia.

Whenever I rewatch the video, I cannot stop smiling. I think Father Bosinio would have liked that.

'Uncle Luke says he is a certified ice bear.'

'What is that?' We are bored silly and the unexpected rain shower in May has trapped us in doors. Adam and I have been chatting online for a while now. Khanyi and Keeya have gotten into an argument that has livened up the street for a bit. All is quiet now, but Khanyi has not yet come online to give us an update on the fight.

'He says he can swim in winter. He swam in the ice in Greenland and in Canada.'

'That cannot be right. He would have frozen to death. Like a popsicle.'

'No, it's the truth you can ask him yourself. Ice bear people jump into freezing lakes. But they don't stay very long, I think about 20 to 30 seconds and then they drink spiced hot chocolate. He has been swimming in the pool every day. Uncle Luke says it has great health benefits, but Mommy says I cannot swim. Life is so unfair.'

'You can always take a cold shower.' I regret it the moment the words leave my mouth. I just hope he doesn't tell Ms Megan it's me when he gets caught. Maybe she'll think it's Uncle Luke's idea.

'I can do that. I'll jump in, count to ten and jump out again. Are you going to try it too? You must. Say you will.'

'It's not me that wants to be an ice bear. And anyway, we don't have a hot sauna.'

'You can put hot water in the bath. Then it's like a sauna.'

'Do you know how much it hurts to get in a warm bath when you are very cold. It burns like hell. No way I'm doing this.'

After careful online research I agree to Adam's ridiculous plan and also to meet online later to tell how it went. However, it takes a lot of begging, pleading and tears from Adam to convince Khanyi to join in the ice bear experiment, that is after he finally started talking to us since his grumpy departure yesterday. I just hope we can pull this off without Ms Megan finding out.

Captain's log Starship Zacharias

STARDATE 15 MAY 2020 ENTRY 3-058

Captain David Miller reporting for Starship Zacharias. Level 4 COVID-19 lockdown regulations are being followed. As of today, the total number of COVID-19 cases in South Africa is 13 524, the death toll stands at 247 with 6083 recoveries. The World Health Organisation reports 4 307 287 confirmed cases with COVID-19 related deaths at 295 101. The number of countries and territories affected is 216. The worst affected countries are America, United Kingdom and Russia.

Today, we wish to say thanks to the healthcare workers who work every day to care for the sick. Our hearts and prayers are with all who are ill and those who have lost family and friends.

End of report.

YEAR 3, MONTH 5, WEEK 21

LOCKDOWN AND DINNER PARTIES

Captain David Zacharias Log

Stardate 73869.82 Log Entry 232

1. *We are going back to school in June. I have homework in all my subjects.*
2. *Carly's dad is getting better. He is still on oxygen but is more alert. He cannot taste or smell food and is struggling to eat.*
3. *I'm now turning into a morning person. I can't wait for six when all of us take to the road. I didn't know that Mom and Dad had bicycles. It was a lot of fun watching them practice getting road-ready. It reminded me of my first practice. But they did not fall.*
4. *Mom is stressed since Dad mentioned that he will be going into the office, starting next week. She is even fighting with him.*

'I'm glad the teachers have given us homework, now Mother and Father will be off my back.' Max pushes his fingers through his too-long hair; it keeps getting in the way. Perhaps he should tie it into a man bun like Adam, but I don't think it will be a good look for Max. It has taken a lot of pleading and begging before Dad agreed to let me go with him to the shops to meet Max. Now we are keeping a safe social distance, each in our own vehicle chatting through the open windows.

'Do they still want you to join a home school centre?'

'Yes. They are not moving on that one. What am I going to do? I don't want to leave school.' He looks pretty depressed with his head resting on his arms.

'Perhaps you can do both, like extra-curricular activity. I take extra classes after school. It can be your extra classes.' I don't like the idea of going back to school without Max.

'That is ten to eleven hours of school each day. When am I going to do homework and sleep?'

'Do you have to take all the subjects?'

'I don't know.'

'Did you even check? What's wrong with you? You usually have all these great ideas.'

'I don't know. I'm just tired, I guess.' He does look down and seems a bit thinner too.

'Well, check it then. Perhaps you can only take the subjects you are going to take in Grade 10.'

'Mmm, okay. But I don't think it will work.'

I'm getting more and more worried. This is not the Max I know. He also did not join in on the last two Starship Reports. Babi said he was sleeping. 'Max, are you okay?'

'Yes. Just tired.' He is silent for a while. 'I miss my family. I love Babi but I miss them. I was hoping they would come home but now Mother says they have to stay until the travel ban is lifted. Mika is so lucky to have them. He sees them every day.'

I always thought that Max was okay with his parents gone all the time. 'Do you talk to them a lot?'

'Mostly Mother. Father is always busy with research or meetings. It must be nice to have your dad home all the time?'

'Sometimes not so much, Dad can be very strict. It's easy to get into trouble when he's at home. He always seems to know when I'm doing something wrong, like goofing off or when Amelia and I are fighting.'

'But at least he's there, you can talk to him.' I do not know how to answer him. 'Do you and Amelia fight a lot?'

'No, not really. Only when she wants me to do stuff I don't like.'

'Like what?'

'Going to the gym. Joining her cardio class, changing my clothes, you know.'

'Huh. You didn't want to go to the gym?' Max sits up. 'If you haven't joined the gym we wouldn't have met and become friends. I'm glad she won the fight.'

'Hey, she didn't win the fight. Dad put his foot down. And we met at the rugby, remember. Jaco was ready to hit you for just talking to us.'

Max is smiling now. 'I remember. You were so worried about the game. But I already decided to be friends with you, that's why I choose Weston High instead of West Ridge.'

'Then you have to stay in Weston High so that we can be friends forever. I'll help you with the research, call me this evening and we do it together. To which school did Boerseun go, do you know?' Last year when playing rugby, a ginormous kid in the fourth team wanted my eight-man spot in the third team and whenever I had the ball he would tackle me into the ground. Once when we were scrumming, he actually growled at me. I'm not looking forward to meeting him again.

'You still scared of him?'

'You would be too! He growled at me like a wild dog. He went like grrrr. You could see his teeth!'

When Babi comes back to the car, Max seems more like his old self. Making jokes and thinking up plans for when lockdown ends. She smiles and pushes his hair back. 'Maximillian, you need a haircut.'

'Nope. I'm going to be a Viking, with horns and everything. Davey, you should also grow your hair.'

'There is no chance – Dad does not believe in long hair. I could always ask him to cut yours.'

'No way – I'm growing it.'

'You'll look like that elf in Lord of the Rings, whatshisname.'

'I don't look like an elf! I'm a Viking. Babi, do you know the elf's name?'

'I don't know, but we can watch the movie on Netflix this evening. I would like to meet the elf you look like. Put on your seatbelt.'

'I'm a Viking, not some silly elf. Does he have wings?'

'Who has wings?' Dad is sanitising his hands before getting into the car.

'The elf that looks like Max. The one in Lord of the Rings. Do you know his name?'

Dad shakes his head. 'You have to ask your mom. Arms inside. Miss Babi and Max, until we meet again, keep safe.'

I waited until Dad has cleared the parking area. 'Dad, I think Max is very lonely – he seems so sad and misses his parents a lot. He's not the same anymore.'

Dad frowns at me, 'What do you mean not the same anymore?'

'Max is just different. He doesn't want to do anything. He used to make these plans and now he is just like whatever. Disinterested and tired all the time. He doesn't even do the Starship Report anymore. I think he misses his dad the most. He says his brother Mika is lucky to see them all the time. And they are not coming home until the travel ban is lifted. When will that be Dad?'

'I don't know Davey.' Dad shakes his head and checks the intersection before crossing. 'Babi mentioned that Max is having a hard time. He was usually so busy with school and with other activities, so he didn't have time to miss his parents. But COVID has changed that.'

'Max's dad wants him to go to a home school centre because the government schools are not providing a proper education and he is falling behind. If he goes to home school, I'll never get to see him, and we will not be friends anymore. He'll even be lonelier.' The thought that Max would not be at school scares me and makes me sad. I stare out the window at the deserted streets. Even the shopping centre's parking area isn't that busy. 'Can't you talk to his parents?'

Dad doesn't answer immediately. He's slowly navigating the once busy streets and for the first time I notice that the leaves have changed into their autumn colours; yellow, orange and a purply red. I like the rustling and crunchy sound that the leaves make when we drive over them.

'David we cannot go against his parents, but Babi is also against it. Maybe if we all work together, we can find a solution that works for both parties. In the meantime, be a good friend to Max and try to get him more involved, not only doing homework together.'

'But we cannot do anything together, we are still in lockdown. He lives too far away to go biking with us.'

'Let's ask your mother, she will definitely know. And before you rush into the house…'

'I know Dad – SANITISE. Mom won't make me shower, will she? I stayed in the car the whole time. I didn't take off my mask. Promise. Not even once.'

'David, do what your mother asks. She is just worried.'

By the time we close the garage door, Mom is waiting for us. Sanitising spray at the ready, yellow gloves and blue mask. We put the bags outside and hold out our hands. Two sprays and she watches with hawk eyes to see if we do a good job rubbing the spray all over. I take off my jacket and hang it on the hanger in the sun. Next are my shoes, neatly stacked on the shoe rack in the sun. Happy that our outer clothing is hanging just right, Mom advances on the groceries. She sprays, we wipe.

'Davey, underside of the milk bottle too.' A glance at Dad and I wipe the bottle again. Dad takes it from me and carefully places it on the sanitised table. Once the groceries have been sanitised, we are allowed inside. 'Go wash your hands and face, Davey. Hank, you take a shower downstairs please. You don't know what you have been in contact with.'

'Yes, Mom.' I hope that Max appreciates all the trouble I must go through just to see him.

'I have an idea to help Max,' says Amelia 'We can have a dinner party.' I nearly choke on my delicious orange chicken. Mom has gone all out for dinner. Tonight, it is wild rice, green salad with parmesan shavings and toasted pine nuts, cooked sweet carrots and the highlight, stuffed chicken breast cooked in a mixture of orange, naartjie and lemon. It is golden, tender, and juicy. And it was my next-to-last bite that nearly went the down the wrong way. It would have been a huge loss.

'Did you forget that we're still in Level 4 lockdown? They cannot come to dinner. It is just a stupid idea.'

'David, that is not a nice thing to say. Let's hear your sister out. Our options are limited, and we'll have to think out of the box to find a solution to help Max.'

'Yes, Dad.'

Amelia carefully arranges her knife and fork on her plate before she lets us in on her crazy scheme. 'Like I said. We invite Babi and Max for a dinner party, not a physical one but a virtual one. Everyone makes the same food and at dinner time we log into Zoom or Teams and eat together. We can invite Carly and her mom too. Carly says her mom is not doing too well, she is so stressed out about her dad that she is not eating or sleeping properly. Perhaps a party will take her mind off things.'

Amelia's idea is not so stupid after all. It's okay if Carly comes, Max finds her interesting. 'What food are we going to eat? Max eats different food. Babi mostly makes Russian dishes.'

'Don't worry Munchkin, we'll sort it out. Perhaps each of us can decide on a dish and share the recipes. Then there is something for all to eat. I'll have to check what we have in the fridge. Davey, did you not say that May and her husband are also staying with Max?'

'Yes, Mom. Auntie May's husband is looking after the garden. Are we going to invite them too?'

'I think we should, it would be rude not to.'

It did not take too long for Amelia's idea of a virtual dinner to become the event to say goodbye to lockdown. When I tell Max he seems happy but not overly enthusiastic. He cannot even decide on a dish he would like to see on the menu. This is so frustrating. Sometimes I get so angry with him, but Mom says I must be patient and not fight with Max when he is like this. I must give him time; he'll talk when he's ready. I hope that when school starts, he'll be his old self again. It seems that for now his dad has accepted Babi's proposal that Max takes extra classes online to make up for lessons lost in Maths, Technology and Economics.

Then I let it slip that we are having a special dinner with Max and Adam explodes.

'It is always Max now! You even invited him to play in the orchestra. It was only for me and you. I'm your best friend, not Max. You even told him about the ice bear! How come he's invited and I'm not? I'm not going to talk to you. You're not a good friend!' And he logs off before I have a chance to explain. I type him an email, but he doesn't respond. So I WhatsApp him.

Adam, you're my bestest friend. The dinner is to help Max. It was Amelia's idea and Mom and Dad said we had to. Ms Roux said we need wind instruments and Max plays the trumpet. It's only for lockdown. He's not taking music lessons with us. You said the ice swimming is good for mental health, and energy and everything. He's not feeling well, so I had to tell him.

I wait ten whole minutes, but Adam is giving me the silent treatment. I must think of something else. Then I have a great idea.

Adam, you are not following the rules. Do I have to teach you everything? When your big brother talks to you, you must respond. You can only ignore your older brother once, that's what the rule says.

I can see Adam is online, and he has read my message but isn't responding. I have to up my game. Being a good friend takes a lot of work. I wish that Adam and Max could get along. This is tiresome. How does Amelia do this, she has lots of friends.

You are my little brother. Remember the guys at the park thought you were my brother until Khanyi said you are the neighbour's kid. I told Max that you are my first ever friend and my little brother.

I wait for what seems like forever and then I see him typing.

Can't I be your best friend and brother?

Yes, my bestest friend and brother.

And Amelia.

???

What's the rule for Amelia? For ignoring her?

Oh, she's a girl. Three times like Khanyi does with Remo. Anything more than that and she'll call in the parents.

Can I come to dinner? I'm family.

So sneaky…

Yes, and Uncle Luke and Ms Megan. Mom says the male company is outnumbered. Let's invite Khanyi too. It will be fun.

Mom didn't say anything when I told her about the slip-up with Adam and that Khanyi and his family are also invited. She just said that it is okay since she invited Tannie Kotie, and Dad asked the Stegmans. By the time Saturday arrives, the whole Starship Report team has been invited to dinner. Even Grandma Edith and Grandpa Heinz. Khanyi invited his friend Jabu from the village and his mom and dad. Since there are so many people and recipes, we picked what we like and will make only those dishes. Mom says I can make Babi's fish dish since it is an easy recipe. Carly's Mom is also making the fish since she's not a good cook and Carly's too impatient; she believes in ready-made meals and tins when it comes to cooking. Amelia says she wants to try the chakalaka that Jabu's Mom sent in. It has beans, bell peppers, onions, tomatoes and lots of spices and chillies. Mom told Amelia to go easy on the chillies. Adam said that Aunt Mabel is not making anything. Uncle Joe said he will do the cooking.

YEAR 3, MONTH 5, WEEK 22

GOODBYE LOCKDOWN LEVEL 4

Captain David Zacharias Log

STARDATE 73889.11 LOG ENTRY 233

1. *Starship Commander Cyril Ramaphosa says we are going to Level 3 from 1 June 2020.*
2. *Still not sure when I'm going back to school. Dad says is looks like only in August. Amelia is starting on the 8th of June.*
3. *Mom is still stressed about Dad going back to work. Dad says there will be no other employees the first week; only the COVID committee people to get the office ready. But I'm still scared. I do not want him to go.*
4. *Dinner party this Saturday.*

'Hank, why does it have to be you? Why can't someone else go back first?' Mom has been after Dad since the first notice came through that essential services are returning to work. Dad is an engineer and involved in water and sanitation projects, which are essential services. Mom is taking out her frustration and anger, loudly hammering in the nails on the mezzanine floor.

'Why is Mom so angry?'

Amelia puts down the varnish and the paint brush and pulls at her mask, not that the mask is any help against the strong chemical smell. 'I think she is just scared; you know. People are getting sick whenever they are together because there are always a few not following the rules.'

'But… Dad said he will be careful. He said there are a lot of rules, and he is going to make sure everyone follows them. He will be safe, won't he?'

'I don't know. We'll have to pray that Dad doesn't get sick or make Mom sick. We must also follow the rules to keep Mom safe.'

'I don't want to go to school anymore. I'm scared. What if Dad dies…'

'Don't say that! Ever! Do you hear me. We cannot stay at home forever. We must follow the rules and if we follow the rules then Mom and Dad will be safe.' I can see that Amelia is scared too, her eyes look so big and she's frowning. A familiar twinge hurts my stomach.

'Amelia, Davey, keep moving with the varnish or else there will be a line – it is the quick-drying type. Keep painting while talking.'

'Yes, Dad!'

Dad has been going to the office on and off, once or twice a week since we moved to Level 4. He only goes in from 9 – 3 pm and it is mostly to supervise the cleaning of the office and help with space planning since the employees will have to observe social distancing. They also had to change the windows so that they can open them for ventilation as they may not use the aircon. Dad says it is not a regulation aircon. Mom says people will be cold since it is winter and will use the aircon. Dad says it has been disconnected. Mom just snorted and ignored his reassurances. From the 1st of June, he will be going back to the office full time and he has been pushing us to finish the mezzanine floor before then. We have been lining up every afternoon, ready for when Dad is back from the office. Mom says it is good that we are working outside, but Dad still needs to take a shower the moment he gets home. And then again once we're done working on the floor. That is too much showering in my opinion.

It is strange how something as simple as a dinner with friends can become something extraordinary in lockdown. The excitement of the dinner party has been building during the week, on Friday and Saturday it was all everyone was talking about after the Starship Report. The food they are going to make, the best wine to go with chilli, beef and fish dishes, the dessert they are serving and even the clothes they are going to wear. We are dressing up. I have to wear a shirt with long sleeves, but Amelia said I can roll up the sleeves and I don't have to wear a tie.

Mom is going all out with her special white plates with the gold trim and the good cutlery. I'm so tired of polishing knives and forks. We even had to dust and clean and vacuum the dining room. Mom cuts fresh flowers from the garden for a centre arrangement. And I'm not just talking about a few flowers in a vase.

'Mom, you know it's a virtual party, they are not going to see the table. Only our faces.'

'It's a special occasion and it's for us. Let's enjoy the good china, it does not do anybody any good while sitting in the cupboard. Also wipe down the glasses.'

'I'm not touching those. They are Grandma Edith's glasses. Amelia can wipe those. Are we going to have wine? Can I have a sip?'

'Only if you wipe down the wine glasses.' Mom holds out the white cloth, daring me to take it in exchange for a sip of wine.

'Okay, I'll do it. But I want my own glass.'

'Deal!' And Mom leaves me to the nerve-racking task of polishing Grandma Edith's crystal glasses to their full sparkling splendour. Fifteen minutes later, I place the last long-stemmed wine glass to the right of the water goblet which is closest to the knife. Between all the white plates and dishes on the white tablecloth, the dark green water glasses shimmer like jewels in the afternoon sun, outshining the golden knives and forks. But they are not the most beautiful. That honour goes to the dessert wine glasses, standing proudly on their own special tray on the sideboard. I've never ever seen them being used. Ever. I tiptoe over and marvel at their fairy-like beauty. They are small, less than ten centimetres in height, delicate silver stems ending in a lacework of dainty silver leaves and flowers cupping a dark blue glass bowl. And when the sun catches them just right the blue shimmers and glows like fire between the silver lace, casting blue and silver lights onto the wall.

My phone has been going crazy, everyone is sending pictures of food and tables. Adam's mom has opened their formal dining room and has ordered Adam to dress in his church clothes. He's even going to wear a bow tie. Khanyi says he is wearing a black shirt with a mandarin collar. I have no idea what that is. When I ask, he says wait until dinner. Max says he'll be wearing a waistcoat, and Babi is putting up her hair. I think I'm going to be underdressed in my white church shirt with the thin black stripes, but I'm not going to wear a tie.

'Okay, Davey, you go get ready. When you are done, we will finish the side salad and the appetiser.' I've just finished helping Mom putting the last of the dishes in the hot drawer. Our simple supper with Max and his Babi is now a three-course formal dinner. The moms have been swapping out ingredients, recipes and even dishes (to Carly and her mom). It made me remember our Operation Pin Drop. It feels like it happened a long time ago, but it was only two months ago. 'Mom, this is a lot of food. Are you sure we are not going to get fat? I don't want to get fat again.' Over this past week I've learned a lot about formal dining and stuff. Like a three-course meal has an entrée, a main course followed by dessert and each course has its own set of knives and forks. Even the dessert has a fork and spoon set.

'Munchkin, there is no chance that we will get fat from this one dinner. Most of the dishes are made up of vegetables. The only bad food is the wine and the brandy and cream sauce for the peach dessert. You can put in an extra cardio class if you are worried.' Mom gives me a dimpled smile when she mentions the cardio. She knows how I hate cardio; it's exhausting. I'm never going to like it.

'No thank you. I've sure I've burned enough calories just making the food. I'll only have small portions of each dish. And I'm not skipping dessert.' Mom holds up her hand for a high five.

'I agree, small portions and not skipping dessert. Go, you'll be late and I've to get ready myself.'

'I'm going – I'm going!' Sheeze, this is getting out of hand, I don't think my jeans and shirt idea is going to cut it. But I'm not giving up the Converse, there is no way I'm wearing my too-tight church shoes.

When I get back from a quick shower, a surprise is waiting for me. My boring church shirt has undergone a transformation. It now has a patterned border running down the front and the top part of the cuffs have black edging. I recognise the border; it is from one of Mom's old caftans. The white buttons have been replaced with black ones. Wow, it looks like something Khanyi would wear. I'm going to look good in this! Can't wait to show it off. I stare at the boy in the mirror. He looks tall, his short dark hair slicked back from a roundish face. The untucked shirt over black trousers, the sleeves one quarter rolled up, makes him look slim, he casually puts his hand in the pants side pocket and strikes a pose. For the first time in my life, I want a picture of myself.

Feeling quite pleased, I leave the bedroom to look for Mom and run into Amelia.

'By the stunned expression on your face I take it I look good?' she asks. She looks awesome, dressed in a pastel blue mini dress with bell sleeves. Pearl and rhinestone beadwork sparkle in the low light when she moves. From the top of her blond ponytail falling fashionably over her left shoulder to the tips of her silver high-heeled sandals, she looks like she has stepped from a fashion magazine. 'You look quite handsome yourself. How do you like the shirt? Mom and I fixed it for you.' She starts pulling me by the arm. 'Let's find someone to a take a picture of us.' Still speechless, I follow her down the stairs.

There is no one in the kitchen. I hear voices in the dining room, and for the second time that evening I'm incapable of forming a sentence. I can only stare dumbstruck at my mom in her long silver evening gown. This is not a dress, it's a gown right out of a magazine. It has a beadwork bodice, chiffon sleeves and a soft pleated skirt that sways gently when she moves. Next to her, Dad is wearing a dark, nearly black, purple shirt with tiny pleats down the front.

'Oh, my – Hank, look at the kids! You look beautiful, so handsome. I want pictures and tonight no one gets to say no.' Mom gives me a fierce stare, but her smile takes all the fire from it.

The evening turns magical. I've never imagined people can look so different when all dressed up. Ms Megan in a red satin dress, her hair in a curly updo. Uncle Luke in a tuxedo, both him and Adam are wearing untied bowties. Khanyi, in his mandarin-collared black shirt with the side-closing white bead buttons. Ms Thandeka, looking even more beautiful in a shimmering gold dress. Tannie Kotie, stylish in a purple dress with a high collar. The Stegmans in dark green and gold. Grandma Edith and Grandpa Heinz in black. Even Miss Mabel stuns us all in a formal black dress with red and blue embroidery down the sleeves. The unofficial guest of honour – Max – is wearing a long sleeveless waistcoat with buckles down the front. He looks like a very dangerous Legolas with his long blond hair tied back. Babi and May, elegant in black satin dresses and May's husband a splash of colour in a blue brocade jacket. It takes a bit of time, but once Miss Emily, beautiful in a buttery yellow dress, turns on the music everyone seems to relax and start talking. I watch the people, laughing and chatting on the monitor that Dad has set up. It turns out that Mom is right, we all need this party – to get dressed up and celebrate life.

The moment Khanyi lays eyes on me he can't help himself. 'You look very fashionable tonight. It must be my discerning fashion style rubbing off on you.'

'Is not. You are not the only one with style. It must be Amelia's choice.' Adam immediately protesting the fact that only Khanyi has style.

'I'm with Adam. It has a woman's touch.' Max raising his opinion. I always find it funny that when we are all together, Max and Adam usually pair up against me, Khanyi and Legs when he joins us.

'This is my old church shirt.'

'Is not – I've never seen it before. You have a white shirt and another white one with black stripes…'

'Like I said, it's an old shirt, it just had a makeover.' I don't mind the teasing; I know I'm looking good in my revamped shirt.

Grandpa Heinz taps lightly on his glass, and everyone fall silent. When he has everyone's attention, Grandpa suddenly stands up and his head disappears from the camera. Dad's brother has to scramble to get the camera adjusted while Grandpa waits silently with a smile on his face. He looks smart in his formal tux. He says something in German to my uncle who only shakes his head before sitting down. 'I'm not going to make a speech or make a toast. On behalf of all of us, I want to say thank you to the next generation, which believes everything is possible, that did not take no for an answer when it was important. To the young ones that made us all one big family, who gave us strength and support in these hard and lonely times – Davey, Adam and Khanyi, thank you for the Starship Report. We are looking forward to the next round.'

'Hear, hear.' The guests are clapping, raising their glasses. I can feel a blush creeping up my cheeks, all the eyes are making me nervous, and I begin an intense study of the table decorations. While Khanyi and I hide with embarrassment, Adam has no problem declaring loudly that the Starship Report will go on forever and that they have to keep getting up real early, even when it is dark. Everyone cheered at the declaration and with the attention diverted, I can start breathing again. Amelia lightly pats me on the back and holds out her glass. 'Congratulations, let's toast the Starship Report.' I lightly clink my glass to hers and take my first sip of the white wine. It's sour! Like taking a bite out of a lemon, and I involuntarily do a doggie shake to get rid of the taste.

'How can you drink this? You should have warned me.'

'Years of practice. It's not bad, it is light and crisp with a fresh lemony taste.' But she does take a quick sip of her water. 'Perhaps we should go for a dry rosé next time. One that's not overly sweet but less citrusy than this.'

'No thanks. I'll stick to water.'

Our first course is Babi's fish recipe. I prepared this dish by myself; Mom only showed me how to cut the fish and she set the oven. The salmon is cooked in foil and just before serving brushed with melted butter mixed with freshly grated garlic and a squeeze of lemon juice. For a bit of colour, I chopped fresh parsley from Tannie Kotie's garden into tiny bits to sprinkle over the fish. I carefully measure out one tablespoon so that it doesn't overpower the other flavours. Amelia said I was over the top with all the measuring, but the proof is in the flavour – it's perfect. The salmon is soft, creamy and tastes different with the garlic butter with a hint of lemon juice.

'Well done, little brother. Your fish tastes divine. Now for my dish.'

Our main course is chicken in an oregano-spiced lemon marinade served with several side dishes, one of which is the chakalaka dish Amelia wanted to try. Jabu's mom sent in the recipe. This dish has so many ingredients and spices, it makes my head spin. Mom says it is everyday vegetables like peppers, onions, tomatoes, carrots and beans. I hope Amelia listened to Mom and went easy on the chillies. If she did not, I came prepared with a small dish of yoghurt placed strategically within reach. I needn't have worried, it was delicious, even the beans had lost their blah taste and I enjoyed their new spiciness.

The dinner lasts like three hours, but it doesn't feel that long, we are having too much fun. When the parents start saying their goodbyes, we are the ones begging them to stay longer, but right at the critical moment Adam yawns, setting us all off and the evening comes to an end. But it leaves me with a warm feeling all over, I haven't felt this happy since my first real birthday party. 'Mom, I had a lot of fun and I think Max did too. He was making jokes again. He is much better now. Thanks, Mom.' Mom gives me a one-armed hug.

'I'm glad, Munchkin. I also enjoyed the evening. It was nice doing something normal.'

'And getting all dressed up. I've missed getting dressed up and going to parties.' Amelia spins around, her blue dress fans out, glittering in the light. 'It was fun. You must agree I have great ideas.'

'Don't let it go to your head, it might explode.' Amelia just laughs at me, grabs my hand and waltzes me around the kitchen.

'C'mon little brother, dance with me.'

Captain's log Starship Zacharias

STARDATE 31 MAY 2020 ENTRY 3-074

Captain David Miller reporting for Starship Zacharias.
Level 3 COVID-19 lockdown regulations are coming into effect at midnight.
All members aboard Starship Zacharias are in good health. No COVID-19 symptoms reported to Medical Office Bubbles. Chief Engineer Miller has been visiting the earth bases putting COVID rules in place for the colonists who will be returning to earth. He is instructed to observe all COVID-19 rules very closely.
The total number of COVID-19 cases in South Africa is standing at 32 683, with 1 716 new cases reported from the last 24-hour testing cycle. Star Commander Ramaphosa has warned that the infection rate will now increase again when people start to go back to work. All personnel leaving the safety of their bases must closely follow all COVID rules. You must be very careful and stay healthy – we need you.
The World Health Organisation reports 5 934 936 cases with 367 166 deaths. The worst-affected countries are America, United Kingdom and Russia. Both the USA and Brazil have had more than 1 000 deaths a day. The Russian Federation, UK and Italy still have more than 100 deaths a day.

Today, we wish the personnel who are going outside to work all the best

– please follow the rules. We pray for you and all the people who are sick and those who are sad because people and family they love have died.

End of report.

YEAR 3, MONTH 6, WEEK 23

I'M AFRAID OF ALERT LEVEL 3

Captain David Zacharias Log

STARDATE 73908.41 LOG ENTRY 234

1. *Starship Commander Cyril Ramaphosa says more people are going to get sick now because more people will be outside. I'm scared for Dad.*
2. *Weston sends out a notification that the Grade 8s are starting school with the Grade 12s as they do not share teachers or classrooms. This time, the teachers will rotate and not the learners. There's a whole list of stuff that we must take to school. Extra masks, sanitiser and a parent must sign us in. We will go to school this week, and the next week the Grade 9s and 11s. The Grade 10s have been split into two groups – one group will go to school with us and the other group will start next week.*
3. *I'm scared of going outside. People are walking in the street without wearing masks, they are even walking together. They are not using the sanitiser at the shops. If nobody follows the rules, we are all going to get sick.*

It is Wednesday afternoon, the week before school officially starts again. After the special lockdown dinner, Max has started to join the Starship Report again. He is slowly getting back to being the old Max of before COVID, joking and making plans, especially mad ones with Adam. They seem to be getting along better. Max gave me a horrible fright when he said his father is totally opposed to him only returning to school in August, but luckily Weston decided to return all grades, so his father is okay for now. I'm really glad he is not leaving school.

'Why can't I also join the band? Davey, why didn't you tell me?' Khanyi is pissed off that he is not invited to play in Ms Roux's orchestra.

'It is something that Davey and I are doing. You were not talking to us anyways.'

Since it was my idea not to include Khanyi in the music lesson I silently watch the two having a go at each other. Ms Roux has suddenly decided that we should do an online performance to show the parents what we have learned throughout lockdown. It took a lot of practice, but we are starting to sound like a real orchestra. We will play classical music and pop songs.

'You are mean. You do not even play an instrument. You cannot rap on classical music.'

'Who says I cannot rap for an orchestra. You even asked Max to play and not me. You are rude, and not my friend.'

'Hey, stop fighting. We are going to school next week and will not be able to see each other during the day.'

'I'm already at school. Miss Emmy hasn't stopped with school lessons at all.' Adam is squishing his face between his fists, looking wrinkly and sad. 'She did not even stop once; I had no holiday at all. Not even one day!'

'That's a lie, you had the April public holidays.'

'I had homework!'

'I did too. Remember? That is why the Starship Report started.'

'How is the reporting going to work when we go back to school? I don't want it to stop, it is not as if we are going to see everyone. The borders are still closed, and we cannot travel and meet friends. And not everyone is going back to work.' Khanyi is asking all the questions that have been running through my mind since they announced lockdown Level 3. I also don't want to give up on the report, it makes me feel safe, connected to people.

'I don't know… We must leave for school at 07:10 and the report only starts at seven. We'll never get it done in time.'

'I know! I know!' Adam has raised his hand and is hopping up and down on his seat. 'We can do it after school or in the evenings.'

'That's just stupid. It won't work, people are still at work when we get back from school and in the evening, Mother makes dinner. She's busy.'

'It's not stupid. You don't know either…' And off the two go again.

'Hey, STOP!' I say. 'We'll vote on it.'

'No, that's not fair. You'll vote for Adam because you've known him longer.'

I jump in before Adam can start a fight again. 'Not us. Everybody must vote – we'll ask them tomorrow.'

Turns out everybody votes to keep the report and on weekdays the report will start at 6 am, and over the weekends it will be at 7:15. When we decide to try the new set times it is funny. The people who are still working remotely show up in their pyjamas with their hair still mussed from their pillow, their sleepy eyes tearing from all the yawning. Each is clutching their favourite drink trying to get the engines started, that's what Mr Stegman says each morning when he hides behind the biggest mug I've seen. He has no head, only the big blue mug with the words *Don't talk to me* printed on it. The ones on their way to work eat their breakfast with huge bites. Some of them are quite messy in the rush to get everything done. Uncle Jo even wears a kitchen towel around his neck like a baby's bib to catch any spills. Thereafter some of the others do too. It is quite disorganised. Takes us a week to settle into the new routine. I like it that everyone is still wearing their Starship pins.

YEAR 3, MONTH 6, WEEK 24

A MOST HORRIBLE, HORRIBLE WEEK

Captain David Zacharias Log

STARDATE 73927.71 LOG ENTRY 235

1. *Go back to school – follow the COVID rules.*
2. *Dad's back at work – he is following the rules.*
3. *Keep safe – social distancing, hand washing, sanitising and wearing masks. Not everyone is following the rules. It is scary.*

On Monday, Khanyi tells us while doing homework that Miss Gillian, the library teacher at Weston Primary has not returned to school. She is in hospital; her husband has already died of COVID. I'm sad and angry that such a nice person like Miss Gillian may die of this horrible disease and I would not even have known if Khanyi had not returned to school. On Tuesday, I mention her in my Starship Report. Miss Emmy knows her. Miss Gillian was her student advisor at university. She is only 34 years old, and she and her husband have a three-year-old baby boy.

Space Station Guten Morgen

STARDATE 10 JUNE 2020 ENTRY 3-084

First Officer Edith Miller reporting on behalf of Station Commander Heinz Miller.

Commander Miller is showing some COVID symptoms, slight fever and sore throat.

He has placed himself in self-isolation for the next week. We wish him a speedy recovery.

Other Station personnel are all in good health.

It feels as if I've been suddenly hit in my stomach, my breath whooshing out. I have trouble breathing, I feel lightheaded. I hear Grandma Edith reading her report, but I cannot concentrate on her words. I watch her steely resolve, her emotionless expression while delivering the report. How can she be so cold? I'm angry at her. Does she not care that Grandpa is sick? It's only when she stacks her papers together that I notice the trembling in her hands, the nervous smoothing of her hair. Touching and pulling, smoothing it back in place. For the first time I notice that she is even slimmer than before. Her high cheekbones are standing out more, her eyes have dark shadows underneath. She looks tired.

At school I get into a shouting match with a tall boy and his friends because they are wearing their masks underneath their chin and not following the rules for social distancing. When I ask them why they are not following the rules, they laugh at me, saying that kids cannot get COVID. The adults should fear the kids. Then some other kids join in and Esha, whose aunt has died, starts to cry, and keeps saying that they are heartless. They laugh at her, making her cry louder. Nobody can comfort her properly, we just touch her back and shoulders, then quickly sanitise. Mr Carter calls me the instigator and sends me to cool off outside. Esha suddenly bursts from the classroom and runs down the steps in the direction of the school gate. After a long while she comes back and sits down on the steps a metre or two away. She's not crying anymore, just curls into herself, rocking slowly back and forth.

'I'm sorry, Esha. I didn't mean to upset you. I was… angry.'

'It is not your fault. I'm angry too. They are not following the rules. They are so cruel! How can they be like that?' I have no answer for her. We stay sitting quietly until the bell rings and Mr Carter leaves to go to the next class.

On Friday, a substitute teacher shows up for Mr Carter's class. He has tested positive for COVID. Everybody looks at the tall boy accusingly and he glares right back at us.

Grandpa is not getting better. He continues to log in during the week to listen to the Starship Report, but doesn't say anything. On Friday, he switches on the camera for a short while to say hello. He looks old and tired. And small in the big bed. He tells us to keep going, everything will turn out okay. He smiles at us, his blue eyes crinkling at the corners before he logs off again.

On the 13th of June 2020, the South African government reports that the total number of confirmed COVID-19 cases in South Africa is 65 736. On this date, a further 69 deaths occurred of which 24 are from Gauteng. One of those 24 is Miss Gillian. Little Johan is now an orphan. I wonder how many other kids have been made orphans because of COVID.

YEAR 3, MONTH 6, WEEK 25

HOME AGAIN

Captain David Zacharias Log

STARDATE 73947.01 LOG ENTRY 236

1. *This week we are having school online. Amelia's Economics teacher has also fallen ill.*
2. *Dad must work two weeks before he has a home week.*
3. *Still following the rules: social distancing, hand washing, sanitising and wearing masks.*
4. *I'm angry all the time. I hate all the selfish people that do not follow the rules.*

Captain's log Starship Lebombo

STARDATE 15 JUNE 2020 ENTRY 3-089

Captain Khanyi Mpilo Mbulazi reporting. Present is First Officer Simi, Officer Nonhla, Chief Operations Officer Thandeka, Enlisted personnel Remothabhile.

Chief Operations Officer Thandeka reported that on School Station X32 another two teachers have taken ill, bringing the total to five.

Ballet teacher Mr Marc-Ray Kirk has been transferred to a step-down facility and is doing much better.

We are however sad to report that retired Principal Adèle Kissinger has died on Sunday evening. She was 78 years old. She leaves behind her daughter and son, four grandchildren and two great-grandchildren. Chief Operations Officer Thandeka has requested that parents must please educate their children on the dangers of not following COVID protocols. The death rate for high school teens is increasing. Five teenagers have already died of COVID.

End of report.

While observing the one minute of silence for the dead – Principal Kissinger, Miss Mollie from Miss Mabel's knitting club and Miss Annetjie who helped Tannie Kotie make pins, I suddenly realise that Khanyi must be really scared – although his mom is the school principal, she also teaches classes. More and more teachers are falling ill. I've watched him waiting at the gate each afternoon for his mother to return. He will only log in once he knows she's okay. Where he previously resisted being hugged by his mother, now he's the one giving her a hug.

I'm not complaining about Mom's COVID rules anymore. I'm now aware that we could carry the virus home with us. I do not moan when it is my turn to hang our school blazers in the sun. I now carefully clean my school shoes and leave them at the front door. I make sure to wash my hands and put my school clothes in the laundry bag. Amelia has asked Mom not to wait on the stoep anymore and for us to eat lunch on the back stoep with all the windows open. Mom sits at the head of the table and the two of us squeeze in at the bottom end, keeping a safe distance from Mom.

Tuesday, 16 June is a public holiday, National Youth Day. This day commemorates the sacrifices of the youth in the 1976 Soweto Uprising and brings attention to the needs and rights of the youth of today. All of us are home, even Dad has taken the day off. But none of us are in a celebrating mood. After a quiet breakfast of oats with blueberries, almonds and peanut butter, we clean the kitchen and go and hide in our rooms again. I don't know what to do, I'm bored, I do not want to do anything, so I lie down on my bed staring at the ceiling. The recovery rate in South Africa is 54,2%. I check Germany's recovery rate; it is at 95.09%. Grandpa has a good chance of getting better.

'Amelia! Amelia, look, Grandpa has a good chance of getting better. Germany has a 95% recovery rate, which means that Grandpa is more likely to get better. And what are you doing?' Amelia is sitting cross-legged on the carpet, her eyes closed, her hands on her knees and her middle fingers and thumbs making a circle. She is wearing what looks like gym clothes. 'What is that music playing?' The music is slow, like some kind of flute or violin, it just drones on and on without a real tune and there are sounds of birds and water.

With a huge sigh, Amelia switches off the music and opens her eyes. 'I'm trying to meditate. You should try it too.'

'Is that not what monks do? Is Mom okay with you doing this? This is like a religious thing is it not?'

'No, it is a relaxing thing. Yoga, remember. Anyone can do this. You should try it. Sit down. I'll show you how.'

'I don't want to. Did you hear that Grandpa is going to get better?' I show her my phone. 'Look, it says that for people over 70 the mor… mortality rate is 20.5%. Is mortality death?' I'm getting worried that Amelia is not sharing my joy and belief that Grandpa is going to get well. 'Aren't you happy? Father Bosinio said we should have faith. I'm going to tell Mom.' I do not get a chance to tell Mom. When I run into the kitchen Mom is hugging Dad, telling him that everything is going to be okay, but her face is so pale and she looks scared. 'Mom, what happened? Is Grandpa, okay? Mom… Mom? Dad?'

It is Dad who tells us the bad news. Amelia has followed me downstairs. Grandpa was rushed to hospital as he was having trouble breathing. He's been placed in ICU. Uncle Matthias will keep us updated as he is at the hospital with Grandma Edith.

I do not remember much after that. I think I cried. I vaguely remember falling asleep on Amelia's bed listening to her strange yoga music with the sounds of birds and water. But the next morning I wake up in my own bed. I go to school, I come home, I ride my bike, I do homework. I go to bed. I wake up, I go to school. I feel nothing. Even when Dad comes home early and lies down in the workroom, I don't feel anything. Not even when Mom tells us that she is putting herself and Dad in self-isolation and that Amelia is in charge. I go to school. I hang our blazers in the sun, clean our shoes. I do whatever Amelia tells me to do. I cut an oxheart tomato on a wooden board and eat it with mozzarella on an English muffin for lunch. We eat the food Mom has put in the freezer. I leave trays of food for Mom and Dad at the door. I collect barely touched plates and scrape the leftovers into the compost bin. I live like a zombie until 24 June 2020.

YEAR 3, MONTH 6, WEEK 26

HEINRICH MILLER

Captain David Zacharias Log

STARDATE 73966.31 LOG ENTRY 237

On Wednesday, 24 June 2020 at 20:12 in the evening, Mom calls us on our phones to come downstairs. I listen to her telling us that Grandpa Heinz is dead, he has died in his sleep. Grandma Edith has collapsed and has been put under sedation. At first, I feel nothing. Then it feels as if I'm burning up. I'm angry, I'm furious, I'm mad. I shout at Mom demanding to know why Grandpa Heinz had to die, he was a much nicer person than Grandma Edith. Words keep spilling out of my mouth, I tell Amelia that she is the reason Grandpa is dead, because she did not have faith. It is her fault. Then she slaps me, once, twice.

'Snap out of it! Grandma Edith is Dad's mom! How can you even say something like that!' She keeps shaking me, my head flopping around. Then Mom is there, she hugs us close, not letting go even when I push at her embrace. Mom just hangs onto us. I smell her soap, the flower-scented shampoo she uses, and the ordinariness cracks the wall I have built around my heart and I quietly start to cry. Mom finally lets go and pushes us away.

'Will the two of you be alright? I have to look after your dad. Davey, don't be angry with Grandma Edith. She is a good woman and loved your grandfather very much. They have been together for nearly 50 years. Just give her a chance and you'll see that she loves you very much too. Amelia, I'm sorry to put everything on you. Call me when you need me.' She turns away but not before I see her tears. When the door closes behind her, Amelia takes my hand and pulls me in the direction of the kitchen.

'Do you want tea?'

'I... I think I would like Milo.'

I watch her fill the kettle with water, switch it on. She takes mugs from the cupboard. They are yellow with white polka dots. 'Do you think Mom and Dad would like a cup too?'

'Dad would rather have hot chocolate. Mom likes Milo.' The next moment the kitchen turns pitch black. Loadshedding has started.

'Is there loadshedding tonight? Perhaps it's only a power outage. The water hasn't boiled yet. Check your phone if we are scheduled.'

'I don't have my phone, it's in my room. Eskom said we are on Level 3 so we will be without power until half past nine. Can we use the gas hob on the stoep to boil the water? I'm thirsty and it's cold.'

'I have mugs in my hands. I cannot see anything. Do you know where the flashlight is?'

'Wait here. I'll get it.' Eskom has put us back into the 'good old days' of paraffin and kerosine lamps, candles, and gas hobs. You now need a generator to keep the lights on. Dad has put his foot down – he is paying the municipality for electricity and is not also going to pay to generate his own. I think he is going to lose the battle; the experts say we are going up to Level 6 load-shedding which could mean up to six hours without power in a day.

My eyes have adjusted a bit, but not enough and I walk into a chair, hit a cupboard corner and bump my head on the door. In the dark I can hear Amelia giggling every time I walk into something.

'You're supposed to ask if I'm okay, not laugh at me.' She giggles again. I locate the flashlight and turn it on. Amelia is holding four mugs in her hands and cradling the Milo tin in between her wrists. 'That'll teach you to multi-task at night. You could have been stuck here until the power came on again.

'Stop talking, my arms are starting to cramp.' I rescue the tin before it slips from her wrists.

'Are you done? We have to go to bed. It's school tomorrow.'

'I don't want to.' I keep cradling the now-cool mug between my hands. I don't want to leave the safety of the kitchen and the warm yellow lamp light. It feels cosy and warm. 'Can I stay with you? In your room I mean. Can we keep the lamp burning? I don't want to be alone.'

I fall asleep watching the little yellow flame dancing behind the glass, Amelia a warm presence behind my back.

The next morning, I dress slowly, deliberately in my new white school shirt that fits properly and neatly ironed grey pants. I put on my school blazer and straighten my tie, smoothing it out. Everything must be perfect. I take time to make sure that my Star Fleet badge – a yellow triangle on a white background with a red border – is pinned straight on my left lapel. I comb my hair one last time. I want to make grandfather proud; everything must be done a hundred percent right. I check the photos that Amelia and I have put together for the remembrance minute. Amelia says it is a collage of Grandpa's life. There is a photo of Grandpa in his military uniform, a wedding picture of him and Grandma Edith, another one with him and his two sons. A picture of our last Christmas together and one from my twelfth birthday with Adam and me. I'm sad while looking at the pictures; all the anger seems to have slipped away. It feels different from when Father Bosinio died. At the time I just wanted to hide away, to sleep until everything was over. This time I *want* to do the Starship Report – I want to honour my grandfather.

Amelia shows up at 06:03, neatly dressed in her school uniform her starship pin with the yellow border a lone pin on the left lapel. All her other badges are proudly displayed on the right lapel. She is pale and her eyes are red. She takes her position and gives me a nod. Together we watch our starship families log in. First Mr Stegman – dressed for work, his starship badge pinned to his collar. He is sipping on a travel mug, eating buttery toast for breakfast. Tannie Kotie, followed by Uncle Jo. Then Adam, he was crying in his mother's arms, but when he sees me, he pulls away and puts on his captain's hat. Max and Babi. Mom and Dad. By 06:10 everyone has logged in. Also, Grandma Edith, sitting at Grandpa's desk. She has placed his captain's cap and pin on the desk in front of her. She looks different, smaller, older and lost. Uncle Mathias is holding her hand and keeps looking at her to see if she is okay.

Captain's log Starship Zacharias.

STARDATE 25 JUNE 2020 ENTRY 3-099

Captain David Zacharias reporting. Present is Chief Engineer and Security Officer Hank Miller, Operations Officer Bubbles Sullivan and Social Science Officer Amelia Perfecto.

It is with great sadness that I must inform you of the death of Station Commander Gunther Heinrich Uber Miller at age 77. Commander Miller died from COVID-19 complications on Wednesday, 24 June 2020 at 20:12. He leaves behind his wife, First Officer Edith, sons Hank and Mathias. He was grandfather to David, Amelia, Ella, Mira and

Heini. Grandpa Heinz was a giant of a man; he was over two metres tall. He was a hero to many people. He always said that we are given two hands to be able to help others. He will always be in our hearts. I miss him very much.

We stand in silence for my grandfather, Station Commander Heinz Miller.

End of report.

I don't want to go to school but Amelia says it is better to keep busy. We walk to school on Wednesday. When the teacher at the gate asks for a parent to sign us in, Amelia says there was a death in the family and we sign in ourselves. We do the same on the Thursday and Friday. I'm tired all the time and do not want to do anything. I wish it was the weekend already. Dad is not feeling better. It has been a week now.

Friday evening, he suddenly contacts me via Teams. I'm so happy to hear his voice although he sounds out of breath.

'Hi Dad. It is nice to see you. Are you feeling better? When will you come out of isolation? Is there anything special you want to eat? Amelia and I have put the third coat of varnish on the floor. She says it looks like a professional job. Do you want to see pictures?'

'Slow down, Davey. If you were not on camera, I would have thought that I'd called Adam.' Dad is smiling. I miss him so much. 'All is well. Not much of an appetite. I'll look at the pictures and let you know my opinion of the job.' Dad is completely out of breath. He stops talking, takes one – two – three – four deep breaths and starts again. 'I'm actually looking for Captain Zacharias.'

'Present Chief – how can I help you?'

'Captain, do you not think that it is time to appoint a new station commander for Space Station Guten Morgen?'

I feel angry when I hear his words. Grandpa has not even

been dead for three days and they want to replace him. How can Dad think like that? He's lost his father! I want to shout, tell him NO, but something makes me stop. I look at Dad, really look at him and for the first time I see him. He could have asked Mom to tell me, but he did not. I can see he is tired and so very pale. His eyes burn bright blue in his white face. His hands are shaking. He is sick but he has shaved, his hair is neatly combed and his pyjamas are unwrinkled. He did all this so it must be important for him. Dad doesn't do games. Even when we are on holiday, playing on the beach or riding our bikes in the park, he is always the one to watch over us. Keeping us safe, watching and warning us when the tide is coming in when we are playing on the beach. or we are riding our bikes too close to the road.

'Chief, don't you think it's too soon?'

'No, Captain. This situation does not allow us the luxury of waiting and grieving too long. It must be done. A ship without its captain is lost.' Dad stops again, taking a few breaths before he can continue. 'Captain, you will have to make the decision. Do not wait too long.'

'Aye, aye, Chief.' Even though I said yes, my heart is shouting NO. I do not want anybody to take my grandpa's place. But my head says listen to Dad. 'Who do you think it should be, Chief?'

Dad tiredly shakes his head, 'Captain, you would know best. Sleep on it for a bit. Over and out for now.' Dad sinks back against the pillows and wipes his face with a heavy hand. He doesn't log off, just keeps watching me.

'Dad, are you okay?' I want to be strong for Dad but inside I'm shaking.

'Getting there Davey. I'm sorry to put everything on you and your sister and keeping your mom with me. I'm going to get well. Everything is going to be okay – we must believe that. You do believe that Davey?'

I do not hesitate to answer 'Yes, Dad' because I've been praying so hard and hoping and holding on to the belief that

Dad and everyone is going to be okay, that I do not even want to think about anything else. My stomach is hurting, I realise my hands are clenched in fists. My whole body feels like it has been wound up like one of those toys and I'm afraid for the day when I'm set loose. I'm scared that I'm going to run and never stop. Dad is going to be okay. He *must* be okay; I still need him.

YEAR 3, MONTH 7, WEEK 27

THE COVID NIGHTMARE CONTINUES

Captain David Zacharias Log

STARDATE 73985.61 LOG ENTRY 238

1. *Appoint a new commander for Space Station Guten Morgen. I must talk to Uncle Mathias first.*
2. *Keep Adam busy, he is driving Uncle Luke bonkers. Not my word. I think it's funny.*
3. *I'm really worried about Dad. I do not want him to go to hospital. We cannot visit him in hospital – he will be all alone.*

On Tuesday morning, Adam, wearing a beanie, puffer jacket and scarf, logs in by himself. Since it is the first time he is all alone, everyone immediately knows that something is wrong. Amelia and I did not have to wait for the report to hear the news. Uncle Luke called Mom on Monday evening to tell her that Ms Megan is not feeling well; she has a fever and her body aches all over. Ms Megan has placed herself in isolation in the downstairs bedroom and will go for a COVID test on Tuesday. Adam is taking it rather well, saying that his mom is still looking the same and she told him to mind his manners and eat all his food. He then reports that that self-appointed Medical Officer Luke is no fun at all. He has told Adam not to put a toe out his bedroom door or he'll lock him in the room. But Adam told him he must put a toe out the door to go to the bathroom, he is not being reasonable. To hear Uncle Luke tell it, it was a full-on scrap with Adam being a hallion and faffing all over the place. Basically, meaning Adam was being Adam and was giving him a hard time. He asked that I please talk to Adam, his nerves are already shot, and he wouldn't be able to cope if Adam fell sick too. The result – Adam can now only go to the bathroom every two hours and may not go downstairs and he must stay in his room when Uncle Luke puts his food on the table at the top of the stairs. Adam complains loudly that it is very cold and windy since the Medical Officer has opened all the windows for the wind to clean out all the germs, but halfway through his report he gets rid of the jacket and scarf.

Captain's log Starship Zacharias.
STARDATE 30 JUNE 2020 ENTRY 3-104
CAPTAIN DAVID MILLER REPORTING.

Coronavirus Report for Starship Zacharias
Chief Engineer Hank Miller is still sick, he is not eating too well. He is struggling to breathe and is using the oxygen machine every day. He says he is working hard to get well. Operations Officer Bubbles is keeping a close eye on him. She is not showing any COVID symptoms but stays in quarantine. All other personnel are in good health and attending to activities on board the ship.

Starfleet released the World Health Organisation report for 30 June 2020. Today marks the six-month anniversary since China reported a cluster of unknown pneumonia cases in Wutan. COVID-19 has now reached 10 million cases and caused 500,000 deaths. As of today, South Africa has 151 209 confirmed cases with 6 945 new cases reported. The recoveries to date are 73 543 – a recovery rate of 48,6%.

While in lockdown our recovery rate was high in the nineties, but now, you are more likely to die than to get well again. I'm scared for Dad, and Ms Megan, I don't want them to die. I just wish this horrible disease would go away.

Although a vaccine has not yet become available, we can still save lives, we are not helpless.
There are things we can do to protect ourselves and others.
Your choices could be the difference between life and death for someone else.

When I read this sentence in the report, I'm angry again at the boy in class who said the teachers need to be afraid of us. I wonder if Dad and Grandpa got sick because of someone's thoughtless actions. Was there an employee that did not wear their mask, did someone go to the shops and not bother to sanitise their hands?

To keep ourselves and others safe we must always keep a safe distance from each other, wash our hands and clean surfaces we have touched, cough into our elbows and cover our mouths. Stay home when you feel sick, and wear your mask properly – make sure to cover your nose and mouth.

And like every other day, I slowly read the names of people who have lost the COVID battle, it is no longer people in their fifties and forties, but also people in their thirties with small children. Jabu's cousin Nandi was 26 years old. She worked as a Sister in a doctor's office.

Let us take a moment to silently honour our family and friends who have lost their lives and pray for the ones who are sick and fighting to get well.

End of Report by Captain David Zacharias.

I've asked everyone to stay online after the last report for the day is done, now everyone is waiting for me to talk. Even Mr Stegman who has been rushing around, phone in hand to get everyone ready for school has taken a seat at the table. He is going to be late for work. I take a deep breath and to avoid their eyes I read what I've written with Amelia's help.

Today is a special day. Although we are still sad about the passing of Station Commander Heinz Miller and worried about our friends and family who are ill. It is my duty to announce that with effect from 1 July 2020, First Officer Edith Miller is appointed to the position of Commander for Space Station Guten Morgen. First Officer Miller is an officer with long years of armed forces experience, she has attained the rank of Major and was First Officer to Station Commander Heinz. We would be honoured if she would accept this appointment and know she will represent the space station well and will contribute much to the community. If she accepts, the position of First Officer will be filled by Ella Miller.

They did not even wait for me to finish talking, people were already clapping and saying hear, hear. 'First Officer, Edith Miller, do you accept your new position?' Grandma does not answer immediately, she looks at us quietly for such a long time that I'm starting to panic and then Uncle Mathias puts his hand on her shoulder. She looks at him and when he nods, she finally answers my question.

'I accept. It will be an honour. I'll do my best. Thank you.'

Uncle Mathias with great ceremony presents the two women with new pins fitting their positions. When he pins the Captain's pin to her collar, she looks like she wants to cry, but she lifts her chin and sits up straight – ready to do battle. The COVID virus better watch out, my Grandma Edith is coming for it. I'm glad I listened to Uncle Mathias when he said that Space Station Guten Morgen needs Grandma Edith and Ella as much as they need the Space Station. When Ella gives a quick smile for the first time in weeks and proudly touches the First Officer pin she has inherited from Grandma Edith, I feel a bit lighter as if things are going to be alright.

By the next day my happy mood has disappeared into a grey nothingness, I'm counting the hours and minutes to Friday.

'Hey Nuke, what's up with you. You haven't even eaten your lunch. Are you sick?'

I'm sitting with Legs and Max on the rugby veld, two metres apart, my lunchbox still unopened on the grass. 'I'm not hungry.'

'What's wrong with you, you spaced out in class too.' Max, who has been lying on his back, is now also up, eyeing me. 'You didn't even react when Bongi sprayed you with sanitiser. You barely said three words today and now you haven't even looked at your lunch.'

'I'm just tired and not really hungry.' Yesterday when I used Mom's banana, cinnamon and nut muffin mix to bake four muffins, one for each of us, I really looked forward to eating them, but today I have no appetite; not even my favourite chocolate apricot energy bar can inspire me to open my lunch box.

'Are you worried about your dad?' Legs is talking around the ginormous vetkoek and mince he has to hold with both hands. He has spread a large yellow and green serviette on his lap and from time to time he uses another one to wipe drippings from his mouth and chin.

'Why have you made the vetkoek so large? It's the size of a plate!'

'My brother was in a hurry to finish the dough before load-shedding started so he made extra-large ones. You want a bite? I can cut a piece off for you. Max, do you want a piece, there is enough?'

'No thanks,' I answer. But Max holds out his lunch box lid and Legs cuts him a generous piece. Not quite sure what the teachers would think about the knife he has stashed in his backpack.

'You're sure you don't want some?'

'I'm sure.'

'I like this. How did you get the dough so crispy? It's still crunchy.' Max licks the sauce from his fingers then attacks the vetkoek again. I watch the two of them finish it off.

'I'm stuffed. Hope Babi is not making a large lunch, I won't be able to eat a single bite. You should have taken a piece home for your dad; it's delicious.'

'I don't know – he is not eating much of anything. Mom has tried everything and he only takes a few bites and leaves the rest. I wish there was something I could do.' I pull at the grass restlessly, breaking off small bits and scattering them around.

'Maybe there is something. It is not scientifically proven yet, but it might help.' Max seems reluctant to share the information.

'What is it? What can I do to make my dad better? You must tell me!'

'Sunlight – UV rays to be specific. Exposure to sunlight might help.'

'Serious? No joke?' Legs is not believing this at all. 'If sunlight cures COVID-19, then nobody would be sick.'

'Nooo, it doesn't cure COVID. Sunlight does however help you get better sooner. It is about vitamin D and feeling better. The doctors have noted that patients who regularly spend time outside during their stay in hospital start getting better sooner. Maybe if Davey's dad sits in the sun each day, he might feel better. When he feels better, he might start eating which will give him more strength and energy to fight COVID. Do you think your dad would give it a try?'

'I think he might and if he doesn't, I'll tell Mom. She'll pester him until he does.' Now that I have a plan, I feel lighter. And hungry too.

It takes a lot of pleading, a bit of crying and a mini tantrum before Mom was even ready to consider dragging Dad out of bed and tiring him out further to sit in the sun which may or may not help him feel better. But eventually, she gives in.

When Dad, leaning heavily on Mom, exits the workroom, I cannot believe this is my dad who is struggling to walk, to breathe, unsteadily trying to stay upright. Amelia makes a strange sound and grabs my hand in a death grip. I'm glad we placed the lounger next to the open door; I do not think Dad would have been able to manage any more steps. He doesn't talk to us, just tries to breathe until Mom puts the oxygen mask on him. After a while his face looks a bit less white and he takes off the mask.

'It is good to see the two of you.' He puts the mask back, takes a few breaths and starts again. 'I'm much better. Must be all the lazing around in bed. From tomorrow I'll do the sun therapy every day.' Mom keeps rubbing Dad's arm. She's smiling but there is no dimple in her cheek.

Mom and Amelia start talking, but I just watch Dad. His blond hair is longer than usual and is sticking to his neck and forehead. He must be feverish; he has red spots on his cheeks and his lips are cracked. He sees me watching and he gives me a smile.

'I'm okay, Davey. The worst is over now. You'll see – soon I'll be inspecting the floor.' He must use the oxygen again. He falls asleep not long after.

We stay outside for an hour, then Mom wakes up Dad and he battles to get upright, his breathing harsh, visibly shaking with the effort it takes. I want to help Dad, but Amelia is hanging onto me, not letting go until Mom closes and locks the door behind them.

'Sheeze, I'm sure I'll never be able to use my hand again! Look my arm is turning blue.' I pull away my arm forcefully from her gorilla grip.

'Serves you right. I needed to make sure that you didn't do

something stupid and then Mom and Dad would not come outside again. We promised Mom we would keep a safe distance.' I don't care that she is right, I just give her a dirty look and run into the house. I hope Dad is going to be okay. When are the scientists going to have the vaccine ready? I must ask Max again. There must be something we can do.

On Saturday morning, a strange sight greets me in the kitchen. It is my turn to make breakfast but Amelia is already busy in the kitchen, but it doesn't look like she's making breakfast. 'Why are you peeling potatoes? Are you trying something new for breakfast? Potatoes aren't breakfast food. And carrots too?'

Amelia wipes at her face with her wrist. She is wearing bright yellow gloves. 'I'm not making breakfast.' Her voice is muffled behind her mask. 'It's still your turn. I want oats like Mom makes it.'

'Why are you wearing a mask? Are you sick? Can't we have cereal? I'm sure there is still bran left. I'll put in raisins and nuts. Mom has ordered almond flakes. Also, some blueberries. You like berries. And Dad doesn't like oats much. I'm sure mine is not as tasty as Mom's.' She doesn't answer me immediately, only keeps peeling the potato to add to the carrots already scraped clean, drifting in a bowl of water.

'Okay. Cereal it is but with everything you've named and yoghurt. But you must add milk too, I don't like it clumpy. And you have to help me with that.' She points the green scraper towards a large oven pan covered with a cloth. When I carefully lift a corner I'm greeted by the back end of a chicken – a whole chicken. I remove the cloth and stare at the naked white chicken in the black oven pan. Now I know why people say they have *hoendervleis* (goosebumps) when they are cold. The pasty chicken does look lonely and cold.

'What are you going to do with this? Where did you get a

whole one? Mom only buys chicken pieces. You didn't kill it yourself, did you?'

'Eeew, that's disgusting! Stop being silly, we got it from the farm.'

'We?'

'Yes. I asked Tannie Kotie to get me a whole chicken.'

I carefully cover the naked chicken before I ask: 'Why?'

'It's for Dad. We are going to make chicken soup. Chicken soup has many health benefits and we are going to make it from scratch and use only the best and freshest ingredients. And you must wear a mask and gloves so that everything is hygienic and germ-free.'

'Where did you read that? And if I remember correctly, Dad isn't much of a soup man, he prefers stew. Maybe you can make him a nice beef stew, you know.'

Amelia is having none of that. She puts down the peeler and grips me by the shoulders, her face is close to mine. 'David, we are making chicken soup and you are going to help. Start making the breakfast. Mom and Dad must be hungry by now. At nine you are going over to Tannie Kotie for the rest of the ingredients. The soup is going to take two hours to make and I want Dad to have chicken soup for lunch.' She pushes me away and starts on the potatoes again. 'Breakfast, now.'

'Two hours!'

'Yes, two hours so get on with it.' Her killer gaze and the potential weapon in her hand convinces me that I'm safer on the other side of the table.

At nine, I ring the bell at the gate and wait for Tannie Kotie. We have not helped in the garden since lockdown started and leaves litter the front yard. There are weeds between the pavers to the white birdbath, leaves are drifting on the water too. It feels like last year, but it's only been about four months. Maybe I should ask her if we can help on Saturdays now that some restrictions have been lifted.

Tannie Kotie comes around the corner of the house. She is dressed for garden work, in blue overalls and her large faded purple hat. Her gumboots are noisy on the gravel path. 'Good it's you. Right on time. Come help me pick the lemons. Your sister says the recipe also uses lemons. The first time I hear about lemons in chicken soup.' She unlocks the gate and waves me in. 'Here are your gloves and you know where the cutters are. You do the lemons and I'll get the kale.'

'She is going to put kale in the soup too. I don't like kale; the leaves are hard to eat and it tastes bitter. Is chicken soup good for you when you are sick?'

Tannie Kotie carefully cuts black tomatoes from the stem and hands me the sun-warmed fruit. 'Here, vitamin C for you. My grandma always said so. Medically speaking it has a high nutritional value with the added spices and herbs. It usually clears the sinuses and loosens the mucus in lungs. Should be good for your father. And your mother. You should make sure she eats well. Cannot be good for her to stay with him all the time. It is only through the grace of God that she is still healthy. Get up there and cut yourself four lemons. Careful of the thorns. I hope your sister knows what she is doing, it is not the recipe that my mother and grandmother used. She is using one from the internet, YouTube, she said.' If Tannie Kotie is concerned and she is all about healthy food and stuff, I should be really worried.

'Tannie Kotie, maybe you can talk to her? You know, just check on the recipe.'

'You know me, I'm not one to interfere.' I couldn't help my snort of disbelief at that statement, but she ignores my quick cover-up cough. 'She must do what she thinks is right. I did offer to give her my grandma's recipe. But you know young people.' She disappears into the hot house all the time complaining about young people.

I carry the ladder to one of the lemon trees growing in her

enormous back yard. There are weeds underneath the tree and I feel guilty for not coming to help in the garden. Even though I'm careful, a thorn still scratches my little finger. I forgot to put on my gloves. I suck my finger to get rid of the burn. When I'm down, I start pulling at the weeds. The soil is still soft and slightly clammy from the dew early in the morning and the weeds come out easily.

'You don't have to do that.' Tannie Kotie holds out the bag and I gather the weeds to put in it.

'It's okay. If you want, I can come back and help in the garden for a while. Maybe Khanyi will come too. I'll ask him.'

'Not today. Come next Saturday. I have people coming. And it's best you keep an eye on that sister of yours. I've put vegetables and herbs on the stoep for you. I've written down my grandma's chicken soup recipe just in case. I've cut up the herbs she wanted, rosemary, thyme and origanum and put them in a cloth bag for you. I've also added basil and fennel and a few mint leaves. Stick one inside the chicken and boil the other one with the bone broth. It is better to use bone broth than those vegetable stock cubes you buy in the shop. Too much salt in those.' She holds out a canvas bag and I drop the four lemons in with the other vegetables. When I take the bag, I need both hands; it is that heavy.

'Tannie Kotie, which vegetables did Amelia want? She already cleaned carrots and potatoes.'

'That one asked for fennel, kale, ginger, and lemongrass. Also, turmeric. But I could only get the dried turmeric from the farmer. The ginger is fresh and the lemongrass too. Remember to crush the stems before you boil it. I've put in some tomatoes, beans and snap peas. The beet is not ready yet. Only one sweet potato. There are tree tomatoes for you.'

'Thanks, Tannie Kotie.' I remember the slightly tangy taste of the tree tomatoes. I wonder if Amelia has ever tasted one. 'I'm going to go now, but I'll see you next Saturday.'

When I get home, I immediately know that trouble is coming my way. Amelia is way too happy to see me and too helpful. 'What do you want?'

'Nothing. I'm just happy that we have all the ingredients now. What is this?' She waves the folded white paper in my direction.

'Tannie Kotie's grandma's chicken soup recipe. Just in case the YouTube thing does not work out.'

'It will work out. I've done careful research and selected the chicken recipe with the highest nutritional value.'

'But will it taste good? That recipe has been eaten by generations of Klopper women. And Tannie Kotie is the health-nut after all. She even sent you bone broth.' We both stare at the brown liquid sloshing around in the glass jar. It has a thin pale coating at the top.

'What is that white stuff?'

'Fat, I think.'

'Are you going to use it. Won't it make the soup oily?'

'I don't know. I wish Mom was here, she would know. I'll have to look it up. I want to show you something, promise not to freak out. But first put on your mask.' And there it is, I just knew that something was up. I follow her into the kitchen.

'What is it?'

'That. We must cut up the chicken.'

'Why?'

'Because the recipe says so. It's easy, I watched a video on YouTube and it is easy.'

If it is so easy, why is she still standing next to me, her hands in her pockets, staring at the naked chicken on the table. 'And you haven't cut it up, because…?'

She gives me an innocent blue-eyed look and a bright smile. 'Because we are doing this for Dad and we are doing it together. Both of us.' She pulls me to the table and pushes me down in a chair. 'First, we are going to watch a video on how to do it and then we are going to … do it. You know, cut it up.'

The video was grisly! The first guy talked about butchering the chicken, popping the bones and you could hear the sounds on the video. He also used scissors to cut through the backbone. The second video was even worse, the woman says we are dispatching the chicken and talks about the best way to break it down. At one stage she told us to place the knife's blade right in the centre of the breastbone to find the keel bone and pick it out of hiding. And then she told us to take the breast into our hands and fold it back, like opening a book. This will force the keel bone to pop up. There was this cracking noise and the chicken split apart and was hanging on by the skin. So gross.

'I'm not doing that. No way. We cook the thing whole. No butchering, cutting, popping… You are on your own.' I try to get to the door but Amelia is hanging onto the back of my jersey.

'It's for Dad. We must do it. You must help me.'

'NO!!!'

'YES!'

'NO. NO. NO.'

'Be quiet. Mom will hear you.' Her voice has dropped to a whisper but is still fierce in her determination to butcher the poor chicken into pieces.

'You were shouting too. Not only me. I'm still not doing it.'

'It will take too long if we boil without cutting. It is already going to take two hours.'

'Why did you have to get a whole chicken? That's why Mom always gets the pieces, it's precut. What if we use the pieces?'

'I told you why and even if we wanted to – they're frozen.' She picks up knife. 'Just hold the chicken, I'll cut it.'

'No way. Weren't you the one not so long ago who needed stitches because your knife slipped in Biology? What happens if your knife slips again? You'll cut off *my* finger – or my whole hand.'

'That was an accident.' But she bites her lip. A nervous habit she has. 'And the chicken is much bigger than a frog.'

I don't move. Trying to come up with something…

anything... not to have to cut the chicken. Amelia pokes at it with the knife. It doesn't move. 'Let me get the pot ready first. We can put it directly in there.' She starts going through the cupboards to find a pot to fit the chicken.

'I have an idea. What if we use the pressure cooker. Mom always says it is much faster than normal cooking.'

'It sure is big enough, but I do not know how to use it and all that pressure can be dangerous. So the answer is no, we're not using the pressure cooker.'

'Mom taught me how to use the whistle pressure cooker, not the new one. I can do it.' She stops looking for a pot. I push her out of the way and pull out the large steam pot. 'And you don't have to cut it at all – it will take the whole chicken.' I put the pot on the table and open the lid and remove the heavy whistle from inside. 'I need hot water. Mom says rinse before use.'

Thirty minutes later, with a lot of help from Google and YouTube, the cooker is happily boiling away. 'See, only 45 minutes. And we did not have to cut it.'

'I hope we did not cut the vegetables too big. Maybe we should have cooked the chicken first and then the vegetables. Perhaps we should have put in more salt. Do you think there is enough salt?'

'You did follow the recipe, did you not?'

'Yes. To the letter. What if it tastes horrible?'

'Then you should have made Tannie Kotie's recipe – not the one from YouTube.'

Amelia folds her arms, eyeing the pot. 'No. Her recipe is boring just chicken, celery, garlic, carrots, salt, pepper and herbs. Our recipe has lots of nutrition and aromatics. It will be tasty and healthy. You'll see.'

I want to spend the waiting time in my room, but Amelia is having none of it. She makes me stay and help her clean up the kitchen. When the whistle blows the first time, she's sure that

I've done something wrong. We nearly start to fight again but after checking Google, she calms down. It seems that she does not believe in my cooking abilities. I should have been angry but I was also nervous using the pressure cooker without Mom. She even made me wait an extra five minutes after switching off the stove, before she let me open the lid. With the billowing cloud of steam came the smell. It is heavenly. First you smell the pepper, then the chicken, ginger, onions. I investigate the pot; it is a clear soup; you can see all the vegetables and herbs. The kale is now small green pieces in the yellowish liquid. The chicken is still whole but small pieces of meat have flaked off. When Amelia uses a fork to test the tenderness of the meat it falls from the bone. I want a taste of this.

'Mom… Mom. We made soup for Dad. It is chicken soup. We made it from a whole chicken.' I put the two bowls on the small table next to the door and take a few steps back. After a while Mom opens the door. She looks tired. 'Mom, you should try it. It tastes really really nice. Amelia found this recipe on the web and we got the ingredients and we made the soup ourselves. Nobody helped. Mom, we used the pressure cooker, just like you taught me.' Mom picks up one of the small Chinese bowls. It was Amelia's idea, because she overheard at our special dinner, that Carly's dad said it was his wife's desperation in giving him only one fish finger that helped him eat. It was a small portion and he thought it would be easy to finish it. And he did. So, she said we should give Dad a small portion. We also gave him mostly soup without any bits and pieces. Only a few to make it look nice.

'This smells amazing. You made it yourself?'

'Yes, Mom and the kitchen is spotless. No dirty dishes and we cleaned the floor.' Amelia has joined me in the passage.

Mom's smile says it all. Just smelling chicken soup seems to give people energy. 'Hank, you must smell this soup. The aroma is delicious. The kids made it for you. Please try a few spoons.'

'Well, bring it in so that I can have a taste.' For the first time in two weeks, I can hear a smile in Dad's voice. And he finished the small bowl of soup. Mom asked for seconds.

'Where were you the whole day? You didn't answer your phone!' Adam does not even give me a chance to say hello.

'Yes, where were you? I saw you coming back from Tannie Kotie. What was in the bag? It looked heavy.' Khanyi is also on my case. Max is not happy that I forgot about our study session in the morning.

'I was busy. We made chicken soup.'

'Why did you do that? I don't like soup.' Adam pulls a face, he's not very keen about the whole soup business.

'Chicken soup is healthy. You give it to sick people. We made the soup from scratch with a whole chicken and lots of vegetables and herbs and it was so good my dad ate a whole bowl.'

'My gogos give me *umdoko* when I'm sick. It's like a porridge and makes you strong. Chicken soup is weak – you need porridge to be strong.'

'Babi makes us potato soup with celery and cabbage when we are sick. She puts in lots of herbs and it is creamy. I should ask her to make it for us. Adam, what food does your mom give you when you are ill?'

'Mommy gives me medicine. Uncle Luke says you have to drink a special milk to get well. He wanted to give Mommy milk but he says the government has put a ban on it.'

'That can't be right. Everyone can buy milk. You must have heard wrong.' Khanyi, clearly puzzled by the story, has stopped pulling his white bread sandwich apart, his full attention now on Adam.

'Perhaps like milk and honey – when you cannot sleep.' Max trying to help.

'Nooo, it is a special one. You buy it from the store that is banned. Wait, I'll go and ask him.' Adam disappears from the monitor and we can hear him yelling to Uncle Luke but we cannot hear the answer.

'So, what is it?' Khanyi asks the question even before Adam is back on screen.

'Milk stout. You buy it from the liquor store. And the government has closed the store. Davey, he says there might be some of the milk still left in the box bench on the stoep. But it must have gone bad by now. You cannot leave milk outside; it tastes bad.' Adam sticks out his tongue to underline the point. 'If you put it in the microwave, it is even worse. It makes this thick gooey mess and it smells horrible. I nearly barfed when I smelled it. Mommy had to throw it away in the outside bin. I always put the milk in the fridge I never leave it out.'

Three pairs of eyes turn in my direction and pin me down. Then Khanyi says what everyone wants to know. 'Davey, go and see if the milk is still there? I want to see what this milk looks like. Go, be quick.'

'Please Davey. Just take a quick look if the milk is there, but don't open it, it might smell barfy bad.'

'Perhaps just take a photo for us. And then you can come back.'

'Okay, wait here. Don't go away.'

I grab my phone and rush downstairs. On the stoep I have to open a few of the built-in benches before I find the milk. There's a pack of are six and I struggle to tear the plastic to get one out. They are going to be in for a surprise. It is not milk at all.

'Did you find it? Did it go bad? Are you going to throw it away?'

I hide the bottle behind my back and sit back down before I answer their questions. 'I found it, but it's not milk at all.'

'It's called milk. How can it not be milk? Do you have a picture?' Khanyi does not find this funny and is impatient for the answer. He is even leaning closer to the monitor, but I've put it out of sight.

Max joins the chorus. 'C'mon, Davey, show us the picture on your phone.'

'I didn't take a picture.' I enjoy their looks of utter amazement and frustration at my lack of cooperation. Adam even slaps his forehead and Max threatens to log off. Then I slowly bring the dark, nearly black bottle with the blue label into view. It's Max who provides the answer to everyone's puzzled look.

'It looks like a beer bottle. Milk stout is a beer?'

'Why does Uncle Luke want Mommy to drink beer? Will it not make her even more sick? What does it taste like? Are you going to taste it?'

'No! This has alcohol in it. It will make me drunk and Dad will most probably kill me again after Mom has killed me first. I'm going to put it back.'

'One sip would not make you drunk. You can take one sip and tell us what it tastes like.' I stare at Max, shocked at his suggestion that I should try it. And of course, Adam is in total agreement.

'Yes, just one small sip. Then you can tell us what it tastes like. Just a little bit, like… like a teaspoon. You should try it.'

Khanyi hammers another nail in. 'Mother drinks beer and she doesn't get drunk. She says it makes you fat. She rather drinks wine. How much is the alcohol content. It is printed on the bottle. Is it like 13%? That is bad and can make you drunk.

'NO, I'm going to put this back. Right now.' I grab the bottle and make for the door. Halfway down the stairs disaster strikes.

'What do you have there? Is it beer? It looks like beer?' Amelia blocks my escape. She doesn't look happy and pulls the bottle out of my hand. 'What are you doing with this? Have you been drinking? Where did you find this?'

'Don't be stupid. I didn't drink it. Look, the bottle is still closed. You can put it back on the stoep. It is Uncle Luke's stash.'

'What are you doing with it then?' Sheeze, this is one pissed-off Miss Perfect. She's shaking the bottle in front of my face while the other is cutting off the blood supply to my arm.

'I'm not telling you. You are such a drama queen and you're overreacting over nothing. You are not the boss of me. Let me go.'

'I am the boss when Mom is not here. And I want to know this very minute why you are skulking around with alcohol in your hand.'

'I'm not skulking or hiding anything – I was walking down the stairs in plain sight, minding my own business and you jumped on me. I'm not talking to you anymore.'

'David. David, come back here – I'm talking to you.'

'What is going on?' Both of us turn to find Mom standing at the bottom of the stairs. Amelia recovers first from the shock at seeing Mom there.

'You should ask your son. He is the one that has been drinking.'

'She's lying Mom. I'm not drinking anything.'

'I caught you red-handed.'

'Both of you get down here.' Mom holds up her hand silencing me. I shoulder Miss Perfect out the way and storm down the stairs. Amelia follows at her usual pace and hands the bottle to Mom.

'Milk stout? Where did you get this?'

'Ask him. He is the one who has been stashing alcohol in his room.'

'I told you it is Uncle Luke's and it was on the stoep.' I turn to Mom. 'I did not drink it. Uncle Luke wants to give Ms Megan milk stout and the others wanted to know what it looks like. I was just showing them and was on my way to put it back when I ran into Miss Perfect. Who unfairly accused me….'

'Enough, Davey. You too Amelia.' Mom looks tired. With a sigh she picks up the bottle. 'Go to your rooms. No talking. I don't want to hear or see you.' She turns and leaves.

'Look what you did. You upset Mom. And now Dad is also

going to be mad at you.' Amelia just can't resist piling on the guilt. I push her out the way and in just as fierce a whisper tell her, 'If you did not make a scene, Mom would not be upset. You...'

'I said no talking. Amelia, go fetch two glasses and a bottle opener. No, make that four glasses.' Mom doesn't talk to me while we wait for Amelia to return. She takes the opener and in one smooth movement opens the bottle with a slight pop. Some foam spurts out, runs down the side and drips onto the floor. Mom does not care; she starts filling the glasses. The one only to halfway and the other three until the foam threatens to spill over the brim. Then she hands each of us a glass. 'Drink.' She takes a sip of hers and then repeats, 'Drink up.' Mom leans against the wall. 'I'm waiting.' By the look of it, she is dead serious. Amelia takes a small sip and puts the glass down.

'This taste horrible. I don't want to drink it.' Mom picks up the glass and hands it back to her. 'Finish it. You too, Davey.'

Amelia and I sit side by side on the stairs drinking the bitter brew. I try drinking it slowly but it still tastes *blegg,* so I decide to drink it in one go but after a three to four big gulps I need to burb, long and low in the back of my throat. Amelia gives me a dirty look and Mom just watches, slowly sipping hers. Amelia tries drinking it fast, but then she also has to burb, hiding lady-like behind her hand. It still feels like hours before we finish the last drop. The bitter taste stays in my mouth and my stomach feels all bloated and windy. Amelia also rubs her stomach and groans. Mom smiles, picks up the half-full glass and leaves for the workroom, where Dad is waiting. 'Wash the glasses and remember the floor too. Put the bottle in the trash. Davey give Uncle Luke the rest of his six pack. Don't use the front door.'

That evening, I learn two more things. One – beer makes you pee. A lot. Two – Perfect Amelia puts on her gown and slippers every single time she goes to the toilet and everything is colour coordinated. Blue slippers with pink ribbons matched with a blue nightgown with pink ribbons on the sleeves with a pink nightie. I, on the other hand, roll out of bed and just go. After running into her for the third time I had to ask and she told me that she has standards to maintain since I had none. I think that Amelia is just super strange, getting dressed up to go to the bathroom every single time.

YEAR 3, MONTH 7 WEEK 28

LEVEL 3 THE NEW NORMAL

Captain David Zacharias Log

STARDATE 74004.91 LOG ENTRY 239

1. *The new normal is not the old normal – that is what the experts say.*
2. *Mom says Dad is getting better. He still cannot walk by himself and uses the oxygen a lot, but he does stay awake longer when he is outside in the sun. I'm still very scared that he will die.*
3. *Ms Megan is also getting better. Adam says she is back to giving orders and checking on his homework. She only sleeps in the afternoons a little bit.*
4. *Station Commander Edith is keeping the neighbourhood on their toes.*

We are getting used to wearing a mask, sanitising our hands and not going anywhere. We must even book a time to go to church since only 50 people are allowed at a time. Our church has two services on Sunday mornings, one at eight and the other at ten. We go with Tannie Kotie to the early service, so I cannot sleep late on Sundays. They have put green and red stickers on the pews and you can only sit in the green rows. Tannie Kotie makes us sit next to the open window and glares at anyone that dares to go near our bench. She once even loudly complained in the middle of the service about people wearing their masks around their chins contaminating the air with germs. I was so embarrassed! I just hope they don't think she's family.

Best of all is that we can exercise from 06:00 to 18:00. Every afternoon, Adam and I go biking. Khanyi sometimes joins us, but most times he just walks with his gogos. The funny thing is that the adults now also have a curfew, they must be home by nine in the evening. It's like they are grounded. I'm sure they are going to remember the curfew when grounding their kids for doing something wrong.

We are still doing the Captain's Report. From time to time, we are joined by the priests from Father Bosinio's last posting. Most of the time they just listen to everyone talking, but sometimes, the younger one, Father Mateo, joins in, asking questions and telling us about life in Bergamo, Italy. They all seem sad and tired. So many people are dying, he tells us that in one day he had to do the death rites for sixteen people in the small locality he serves. When Tannie Kotie asks him how they continue under those circumstances, he says it is the unexpected kindness of strangers that becomes friends, his faith and also Fathers Gascoigne and Petrie who have taken him into their home and treat him like a son. Father Petrie made a comment that had all of them laughing. They all look much younger, more alive when they laugh and for a moment the sadness leaves their eyes. 'Father Petrie says good food and wine.' Everybody starts talking about their favourite food. It turns out that most people like freshly baked bread with butter and coffee if you are South African, the Germans are a bit split between coffee and wine but for the Italian priests it's vino all the way.

And sometimes, things go wrong and the report ends in chaos with us laughing and smiling all through the day. Like the time Mr Stegman went to the bathroom and forgot to switch to mute and we could hear *everything*. Or the time that Uncle Jo was in a rush and he stormed into the kitchen only wearing a towel. That was gross, all that hair everywhere and very little on his head. But the best one and which led to an officer being suspended for a whole week was none other than Station Commander Edith Miller.

The Captain's Report starts off as usual. Only this time, the report for Space Station Guten Morgen is read by First Officer Ella, father's niece. The station commander is nowhere to be seen. First Officer Miller starts her report stating that as of yesterday, 7 July 2020, the total number of people infected with the virus in Germany is 198 765. The death toll in Germany is standing at 9130, an average of 7,7 deaths a day. With twelve new deaths reported today. She says that the health system is coping very well and that travel restriction have been reduced, but that travellers still need to go into quarantine for fourteen days from listed locations. After she finishes her report, Tannie Kotie asks about Grandma. First Officer Miller assures us that Commander Edith is in good health and spirits. But then she mentions with a huge smile that Commander Edith is reporting to the *Ordnungsamt*. When she sees our puzzled faces, Ella explains that the *Ordnungsamt* is the public order police. Like a municipal official dealing with noise complaints, wild animals, assignment of parking spaces, registration of dogs, that kind of things and also social misbehaviour. By then she was giggling the whole time.

'First Officer Miller is there anything you want to share with us?' It is Uncle Jo that asks the question that is burning in everyone's mind. Why does Grandma Edith have to report to the Social Police?

Ella first checks over her shoulder. 'I cannot explain it, I need to show you.' Again, she looks over her shoulder before quickly connecting her phone to the laptop. 'I'll share my screen; the sound is not too bad.'

It's a video of Grandma walking in a street and we can hear her issuing instructions to her small helpers all dressed in masks, gloves and plastic aprons to help pick up litter, and clear weeds and branches. She is watering the high hanging plants. It doesn't seem very funny to me. Then a group of young people lazing around in the sun call out to her and throw their empty beer cans at the kids to pick up. Grandma is having none of that and she speaks to them sharply in German. That is when things start to get interesting. We can hear Ella explaining that the young man who is sitting up is telling Grandma very rudely to take her uptight attitude somewhere else. He is swearing at Grandma! That is when Grandma shakes her head sadly and tells him that he cannot even swear properly, she's very disappointed and it seems that besides training him not to litter, she will also have to teach him a thing or two about swearing.

Ella does try to keep translating but she completely loses it by the time Grandma reaches Agab and the ten thousand fleas from the camel armpits that should make a home in the guy's tiny beard. Mr Stegman is clapping his hands, cheering Grandma on, Tannie Kotie is shaking her head and Uncle Jo and Babi have the same stunned expression as the other young people on the grassy square. The next moment the screen goes blank and after a short break a very stern-looking Grandma appears on screen.

'Space Station Guten Morgen will be logging off. Station Commander Edith Miller signing out.'

We are all left staring at a black screen. Then Uncle Luke puts two fingers in his mouth and gives a loud whistle. 'Way to go Grandma Edith! Where did she learn to swear like that? Not a single f-word and she still manages to tell him off. I'm impressed. I want to learn that too. Would come in handy in my line of work.'

It is Dad that clears up the mystery of Grandma's expertise in swearing. She was a drill sergeant for a few years, and drill sergeants have a large and colourful vocabulary to keep the troops in line. As for the reason why she has to report to the Social Police, it is actually something boring and we hear the next day. The neighbourhood has nominated her to be the COVID-19 reporting officer. She had to register at the office of the Social Police. They gave her training on how to fill in the forms and she received a green reflector jacket that says she is a Regulatory Officer and COVID Volunteer.

The next day Station Commander Edith Miller informed the captains that First Officer Ella Miller has been placed on suspension for a week for disrespecting her commanding officer. Ella later told us that Grandma was not that angry, just embarrassed. She also told us that the rude young man Hans is now a firm supporter of Grandma and is acting as her First Officer when she does the rounds in the neighbourhood. He carries her bag, brings her coffee, picks up information packs from Social Order Police and runs all kinds of errands for her. In the beginning Ella seems to be a bit upset about someone else taking over, but later she enjoys telling us about all the stuff she does in her free time. The Germans can even eat out, she bought herself ice cream with three different flavoured scoops from the ice cream shop. I wish I could have some creamy, smooth chocolate ice cream. I wonder if Woolies still sells that super-delicious yoghurt ice cream, but they don't deliver, only Checkers and Pick 'n Pay does, and there is no ice cream on their online shopping list. I guess it would melt too quickly in the box on the back of their delivery scooters.

YEAR 3, MONTH 7, WEEK 29

SILVER LINING

Captain David Zacharias Log

STARDATE 74024.18 LOG ENTRY 240

1. *Walk with Dad around the garden on Wednesdays and Fridays.*
2. *Busy with exams. I want to score 70% on my language test.*
3. *Go biking with Jennie.*

It is bad now, the COVID infections are exceeding 13 000 a day. On 18 July 2020, the number of new cases was 13 285 and today, 19 July, there are 13 450 new cases. Each morning, while eating breakfast, we listen to the news. I want to switch off the radio, but Amelia says we cannot be ostriches. I have no idea what she means and I'm too tired to ask and my days continue to start with listening to the numbers getting higher and higher. I wish Mom and Dad were here. Mom says that they will finish their 20 days post-infection quarantine soon. Soon doesn't have a date.

'Aren't you done yet?' I ask.

Khanyi is still doing homework, highlighting words on a document. I've been done for ages and he is still at it. 'What is taking you so long today? It is Friday for heaven's sake. Get it done, I want to go biking.'

'I'm nearly done – why don't you help me then I'll finish faster.' He doesn't even look up from what he is doing.

'I'll help, what are you doing?' Adam is still getting dressed in his ninja suit while keeping an eye on the oxygen bottle which is slowly filling with air and is now his constant companion when going out. He has stopped trying to change the adults' minds about letting him out with only a mask.

'Dry your hair first.'

'I'm wearing a helmet, see. Don't need to. I wanna help.'

'You can look it up on Google – it is from the president's office. I'm using his letter of 20 July 2020 to find idioms. Mr Daniels says that politicians are talking in idioms to soften the blows. I must find all the idioms in the president's letter.'

When Adam finds the letter with the logo online, he gets worried. 'You are reading government letters, are you not going to get in trouble? Father says government document are comfi… secret. You cannot just read it.'

'No dummy, it's online and it's for us – see it says *Dear Fellow South Africans*. I'm South African and I can read it. Help me find the idioms in it.'

'I'm not a dummy. I'm not going to help you anymore. You have to say sorry.' Adam turns his back on us and pretends to check the oxygen dial.

'Have your own way, but I'm not saying sorry.'

'Adam, if we want to go biking you must help, you know I'm not good with this. Khanyi just say sorry.'

'Gffm, he has to mean it. You can't just say sorry.' Adam folds his arms and stares at Khanyi, waiting for his apology.

'Khanyi, please just do it. It's Friday and a nice day. Let's go before it starts raining again.' For a moment is seems that he is going to ignore my request and then he gives a huge sigh.

'I'm sorry Adam. Can you please help me?'

'You don't *sound* very sorry.'

'ADAM!'

'Okay, I'm looking for idioms. You should look too.'

'I'm looking.' I start reading the letter again. The first one is easy; the president says *necessity is the mother of invention* but Khanyi has already highlighted that one. 'What about dark cloud?'

'I've done that one already, see *silver lining* and *dark cloud.*' Khanyi lifts the page.

'Not that one, the one before that one. Who is the dummy now?' Adam digging in again.

'If you start fighting again, I'm going to bike alone. My homework is done and I don't need to wait for oxygen.' Two dark pairs of eyes give me a dirty look and then continue to search for idioms. I've given up and start to read the letter. The president is writing about South African youth who are *the green shoots of renewal. They are the silver lining to the dark COVID-19 cloud.* It is about these young people in Langa, Cape Town, who have a bicycle delivery service called Cloudy Deliveries. They are doing shopping for the elderly who cannot go out, and delivering it to their homes. Then in Limpopo, there is 28-year-old Election Baloyi, whose hobby is pizza-making. He has turned it into a business called Rabbit's Pizza and even employs nine delivery people. He is going to open more shops. There is also a woman making masks and a DJ holding concerts online. I could not understand the rest of the letter, it was talking about the economy and small businesses and there were lots of idioms like *leap of faith* and lots of nouns like *rallying cry* and *enterprising spirit* but I like the one about the silver lining in the dark COVID cloud the most.

I guess you could say that Dad getting better is my silver lining.

YEAR 3, MONTH 7, WEEK 30

SCHOOL HOLIDAYS. NOT REALLY

Captain David Zacharias Log

STARDATE 74043.21 LOG ENTRY 241

1. *I still walk with Dad on Wednesdays and Fridays and sometimes he walks round the block.*
2. *Exams are done. I scored 73% on my language test.*
3. *Jennie misses her grandfather a lot. He had been living with them since she was born.*

On 23 July 2020, President Cyril Ramaphosa announces that all public schools will be closing again for four weeks, because the Commission thinks there is going to be an increase in COVID-19 infections. The president says all the schools must close from 27 July 27 to 24 August. But the Grade 12 pupils must return to school on 3 August and the Weston High Grade 8s will return on 10 August. I get one more week of holiday. But I have so much homework it's not a holiday at all. I'm kind of tired though.

Mom and Dad have finally come out of quarantine. The doctor has not yet cleared Dad to go back to work so he is working from home. Mom has decided that three hours a day is more than enough and Dad didn't even fight her about it. He is still sleeping a lot, but he always wakes in the afternoon to walk with me. He says we have done well to keep the garden in order. I did tell him that Tannie Kotie helped and Khanyi and sometimes Adam.

'Not broccoli again! This is the second evening in a row that we are eating broccoli.'

Amelia bangs a lid on the pan and turns on me. 'You don't have to eat it. I'm tired of you complaining about the food. Why don't you make dinner?'

She's looking so fierce that I take a careful step back. 'What's wrong, where's Mom?'

'She has a headache.' Keeping the lid on, she viciously shakes the broccoli in the pan.

'Is she sick? Is a headache not a COVID symptom?' I frantically search for my phone. I don't want Mom to be sick. 'My phone is upstairs. Is a headache a symptom? Answer me!'

'Davey, everything is okay. It's just too much sun and all the stress getting to me.' The moment I hear Mom's voice, I run to her and give her a big hug. 'I'm feeling much better now. Nothing to worry about. It's not COVID. Let's help Amelia make dinner. Tannie Kotie was somewhat over generous with her vegetables. She says the three of you have helped her plant and grow the vegetables. She also brought spinach.'

'So, it's your fault, little brother, that we must eat broccoli two evenings in a row. Your little green fingers did you in.'

I cannot argue with her, I did help plant the spinach and broccoli and cabbages. I just did not think we were going to have to eat them all. 'Did she bring cabbage too?'

'Yes, and cauliflower, leeks, spring onions and turnips. You have been a busy bee. Lucky for you I found a recipe that uses broccoli, spinach and basil.'

It doesn't sound very nice, too much green. 'Is it a soup or a salad.'

'You'll just have to wait and see.' Amelia tuns back to the stove and ignores my question.

'Moooom…!'

'It's a salad, Davey, and we are adding spicy beef strips and peppadews to it.'

'I don't think Dad is going to like it.'

'You mean you do not like it. Dad likes vegetables. You are such a fussy eater.'

'Stop it. Davey, please start the pasta. Not too much this time, a cup and a half will do. Maybe just one cup – there are a lot of greens and we do have beef too. I'll prepare the lemon and olive oil dressing. Perhaps I should add garlic.'

In the end, it was delicious. I did tell Amelia, but she was not ready to make peace. Only told me that tomorrow's supper is on me. She's looking forward to my cabbage surprise. But she is not mad anymore when I wake her up very early the next morning.

I am asleep when my phone rings. I wake with a start and fumble to answer it. I can see it's Adam, but the screen doesn't want to work, I keep punching the green button, but it keeps ringing and I cannot answer. I'm so scared. 'Adam – Adam what's wrong?'

'My throat hurts, can you call Mommy? She doesn't hear me. My head hurts too. My nose is stuffy. Call Mommy for me.'

'Okay, okay, I'll call her.'

'Don't put the phone down, I'm scared. Call Mommy.'

'But you are on the phone. I can't call her.' I don't know what to do. I'm wide awake now but my brain is not working. Adam is sick – he's going to die.

'Don't put the phone down.'

The zombie fog clears from my brain. 'Amelia! I'll ask Amelia. Don't go anywhere.'

'I'm in bed, where am I supposed to go to? Call Mommy.'

'Amelia…! Amelia, wake up. Adam is sick.' Amelia wakes instantly, sitting up and blinking in the bright overhead light. 'Call Ms Megan! Adam is sick.'

'Where is Adam?' She's already reaching for her phone. 'Where is he?'

'In his bed. Call Ms Megan, now.'

'Calm down, Davey, I am calling. Please switch off the overhead light, it's hurting my eyes.' She switches on the bed lamp. I want to scream at her for wasting time and I run to the door to switch off the light. Before I reach it, Mom is standing in the doorway. Dad too.

'What's wrong?'

'Mom – Adam is sick! Is he going to die?'

'I'm not going to die. Did you call Mommy?' I've forgotten that Adam is still on the line. Mom takes the phone from me.

'Adam, honey, what is wrong?'

'My throat hurts. I want Mommy. I'm hot too.' Mom keeps talking to Adam, calming him down. Amelia gets through to Ms Megan. I can hear her calling for Uncle Luke. Then everyone seems to be in Adam's room, talking at once and Adam is crying. The phone goes dead.

'Dad! Dad, the phone is dead. What's going to happen?'

'Nothing is going to happen. They will call us as soon as Adam is sorted out. Calm down and go and put on your slippers.' Dad pushes me in the direction of the door. 'Put on your robe too, no need for you to catch a cold.'

I can't find my robe and grab the hoodie I've been wearing during the day. I struggle to pull on my slippers and eventually give up and run downstairs with my slippers in my hand. 'Did they call? Is Adam okay?'

'No Davey, give them some time.' Dad looks at my bare feet and I quickly sit down and pull on my slippers.

'What's taking them so long? Is Adam going to be okay? Are they going to take him to hospital? He doesn't like hospitals…' Mom puts her hand over my mouth.

'Slow down now. We are going to wait until the kettle boils and then we are going to call, okay?'

'Yes, Mom.' I watch Amelia and Mom putting out mugs and heating up milk for the Milo. Mom's pink gown is only belted at the waist, while Amelia's is neatly buttoned and the ribbon belt tied into a bow. Even the tail ends are perfectly even. How does she do it? And to rub it in she was in the kitchen even before me.

'I'm so glad it is not loadshedding. It would be horrid to wait around in the dark. And without something hot to drink.' Miss Perfect delicately shudders at the thought and cups her hands around the hot Milo.

Dad checks his watch. 'You have about eleven minutes before the power goes out. Best to start lighting the lamps. Hope they get back to us before the cellphone tower's batteries run out.' Mom and Amelia light the lamps one by one, a warm glow building in the kitchen since Mom has only switched on the under-cabinet lights to boil the kettle. 'Davey, go and fetch your flashlight and switch on the little battery lamps on the stairs.'

I want to protest, but Dad looks tired and I swallow my angry words. I'm sure I've set a record for going up the stairs and switching on the little green lamps on my way down. 'Did they call while I was away?'

'You haven't even been gone for three minutes. Just sit down and drink your Milo. They will call when they are ready.' Seems Miss Perfect is worried too.

They haven't called by the time the lights go out. I anxiously watch the minutes tick by, then Mom's cellphone rings. Mom puts her phone on speaker. 'Megan, how is Adam?'

'Much better now. Luke says it is just a head cold. We have given him something for the fever and did a Vicks steam. His nose is not so blocked and Luke made a honey concoction for his throat. Can you believe I do not have any nasal spray in the house. Adam is already falling asleep.'

'Megan, I do not think Luke is qualified to make that diagnosis as a First Aider. It is best to try and get hold of his paediatrician tomorrow. Just to be safe you know.'

'It's okay, I have complete faith in Luke, he has been such a help over the past weeks. I'm sure Adam will be up and about in two or three days.'

Mom takes a deep breath and tries again. 'Megan, although I love my half-brother dearly, Luke is not a medical doctor, please get Adam checked out.'

'Bubbles, don't go ninety on me, but I really am a qualified doctor. I was just acting the maggot, you hear.' Uncle Luke must be stressed if he goes all Irish. But it's too late to tell Mom not to be angry, she does not like being made a fool. She is already giving him an earful, not believing him at all. In the end it was Dad who settled the matter.

'Bubbles, love. I've always told you time and time again that financially it does not make sense that a First Aider could afford to do extreme sports.'

'You believe his story about being a medical doctor? A sports medicine doctor to be precise.'

Dad puts his elbows on the table and rests his chin on his fingers. 'A specialist. Yes. And if I remember correctly, you now owe me R500.' Mom keeps staring at Dad, her eyes all round, not a single word coming out. Then for the first time in a long while Dad starts to laugh. 'I have to say it. I told you so.' Mom hides her face behind her hands, ashamed of being called out. Dad puts his arm around her and gives her a kiss on the cheek. But he doesn't stop smiling.

Turns out Uncle Luke was right. It was just a head cold brought on by Adam not drying his long hair. Ms Megan told Adam that she is going to cut his hair, no more man bun for him and he could not bike with us for the rest of the week. Even though everything ended okay, I cannot forget how scared I was and the feeling that my world had stopped.

For a few days afterwards I have nightmares about Adam dying. I wake up crying, and sometimes Amelia is there, or Mom and one time Dad. But I'm better now.

YEAR 3, MONTH 8, WEEK 31

LAST WEEK OF HOME SCHOOL

Captain David Zacharias Log

STARDATE 74062.78 LOG ENTRY 242

1. *Dad is much better. Tannie Kotie has given him exercises to strengthen his lungs. We are having competitions to see who can blow the largest rubber glove balloon. Amelia wins most of the time, Dad says it's because of her swimming training.*
2. *Mom has decided I must learn how to sew on buttons and do seams. I don't like it but Mom says I must learn to take care of my clothes. I'm not much good at it, but Dad can sew tiny stiches. He says he will teach me the secret of tiny stitches.*
3. *Uncle Luke is still trying to convince Mom not to tell the family about him being a real doctor. It's not working.*

Captain's log Starship Lebombo

STARDATE 11 APRIL 2020 ENTRY 3-139

Captain Khanyi Mpilo Mbulazi reporting. Present today is First Officer Simi, Officer Nonhla and Enlisted Personnel Remothabhile.

All personnel aboard Starship Lebombo are doing well. First Officer Nonhla and Operations Officer Thandeka have put the crew on a healthy eating plan to get rid of the lockdown weight gain. Station Commander Jabu reports that Mr Dumisani who owns the spaza shop is doing much better. His wife, Miss Thabisa is still in hospital and we do not have news. Mr Wandile is out of the hospital, he is going to stay with his son in Howick until he is better.
Commander Jabu says people are still getting sick
but God is taking care of the village and there were no deaths this week. Mr Stegman says his mother, Miss Helen is home and is doing much better. The exercises suggested by Horticultural Officer Kotie Klopper are helping her to get strong again.

End of Report by Captain Mbulazi.

YEAR 3, MONTH 8, WEEK 32

BACK TO SCHOOL

Captain David Zacharias Log

STARDATE 74082.08 LOG ENTRY 243

1. *I don't want to go back to school.*

On Sunday morning, I was the one who switched on the radio to listen to the COVID-19 report. When the news report says that 6 670 new cases were identified, I felt a shiver running down my back. Why do they want us to go to school, all 900 Weston High learners at once when the figures keep rising? Max says it will still be three to four months before the vaccine is ready. Can't we just stay home until they have a vaccine? Or go in on alternate days like we did before. Even worse, South Africa's recovery rate has dropped to 73% and in one day 198 people died. I wanna stay home.

On Monday, 10 August, 3 755 new cases were reported and 213 people died. With the second most deaths in Gauteng, a total of 39. Still, Mom loads us up in the car and takes us to school. I put on two masks and Amelia laughs at me. I ignore her. In class I sit next to the open window. I don't care how cold it is – fresh air is important. The teachers have been instructed not to close the classroom door and tell us to wear warm clothes to school. I wish it was Friday already.

The only fun I've had this whole week was helping Uncle Luke to come up with ideas to convince Mom not to give away his secret. Nothing worked, but Mom has not told Grandma and Grandpa Sullivan yet. I feel sorry for him, Mom is going to get him back good for making a fool of her. I can't wait.

YEAR 3, MONTH 8, WEEK 33

ALERT LEVEL 2

Captain David Zacharias Log

STARDATE 74101.38 LOG ENTRY 244

1. *I just want COVID to be over. I'm tired of everything, the masks, the sanitising and most of all the fear of bringing the virus home from school. I don't want Mom and Dad to be sick again.*
2. *Amelia says we will need to learn how to socialise again. When I told her that I don't want to, she told me I have post-lockdown fatigue.*
3. *I've gained weight, a whole pants size. Mom says the extra weight will fall off when we get active again and I stop stressing about COVID. She has lost a lot of weight and Dad is skinny now. He looks so different now, kind of old and frail. Amelia is, as always, perfect. It is only me that has blown up again.*

Even though I'm so tired of everything about COVID I feel sad that today, it is our last Monday with a Starship Report. From now on we will only meet once a week, on Sundays at four. When we heard on 15 August 2020 that South

Africa is moving to Alert Level 2, we were all happy and relieved that after five months we are getting back to living life again, although with masks and sanitisers. The president said that gatherings of no more than 50 people will be allowed. How did they decide on 50 being the safe number? How do they know that when 51 people are together they are going to get sick?

I checked one last time that my starship badge, the small white triangle with a red border is pinned just right, then I take my place in front of the monitor. Almost everyone has logged in already. I can see the three priests drinking coffee, Mr Stegman already dressed for work, Babi and Max, Uncle Jo and Aunt Mabel, Mom and Dad. At 06:15 I start the last Starship Report for the week.

Captain's log Starship Zacharias

STARDATE 17 AUGUST 2020 ENTRY 3-152

Captain David Miller reporting for Starship Zacharias.
Level 2 COVID-19 lockdown regulations are being followed.
The following personnel are present at the meeting.
Captains announce yourself followed by the Station Commanders.

Captain Adam Sullivan McKenzie of the Starship McKenzie – all personnel present and accounted for.
Captain Khanyi Mpilo Mbulazi of the Starship Lebombo – all personnel present and accounted for.
Commander Edith Miller reporting for Space Station Guten Morgen – all personnel present and accounted for.
Education Officer Emily reporting for Space Station Bumblebee – all personnel present and accounted for.
Commander Jabu Ngabe reporting for Space Station Isaiah all personnel are healthy. Chief Bandile present.

I watch the other stations report in, all five of them. I'm going to miss these people. I take a deep breath and start reading the closing report that I've written with the help of Mom, Dad and Amelia. It makes it special because everyone wanted to say something. Amelia said we need to say thank you to all the healthcare workers, Mom said we should still be careful in the days to come. Dad says we must also report the recoveries, people do get well again. Dad agrees with Mom that we should be careful and told me to include the safety rules.

Today is the start of a new beginning, Starfleet Commander-In-Chief Cyril Ramaphosa has downgraded South Africa to Alert Level 2. It has taken 144 days to get here. During this time, we have lost 11 982 people, many of them loved ones. We are sad that they are gone and we are thankful for the many who have recovered and are getting well. As of today, our recoveries are at 477 671 which translates to a recovery rate of 80%.

We say thank you to all the medical personnel and other frontline workers – police, traffic officers, soldiers, clergy and volunteers who have selflessly taken care of others and have lost their lives.

Starfleet has released the World Health Organisation report for 17 August 2020. The report states that globally there are 21 654 607 people infected, 769 454 deaths and 212 countries affected. Today 6945 new cases were reported. The world recoveries stand at 73 543 which is a recovery rate of 48,6%. The Americas are still the worst-affected region with 11 667 196 cases and 419995 deaths.

We should all remember that even at Level 2, the risk of infection is still high as more and more people are starting to go back to work and attend school and church. We must continue to wear our masks when going out, keep our social distance and sanitise our hands.
We must make sure where people get together indoors that the place is well ventilated.

Before I hand over to the other captains, I want to say thank you to everybody who joined the Starship Report when we asked you in March. Thank you for logging in each day and helping us to honour all the people who have died, so that they are not forgotten.

The next Starship Report will take place on Sunday, 23 August 2020 at16:00 South African time.
End of Report by Captain Zacharias Miller.

EPILOGUE

SUNDAY, 4 APRIL 2021

On Easter Sunday I'm once again standing at the top of St Michael's Avenue with Adam. This time we are not alone. Today there are 24 of us. Each of us is wearing a white T-shirt with the names of people who have died written on it by family and friends. On my T-shirt, I've written the names of Grandpa Heinz and Father Bosinio, some of the names on my T-shirt I recognise from church and school, but others were written by strangers and those I do not know. But I'm proud to carry their memories today.

Max, Khanyi, Adam and I will be in the first group. Following us will be Big H, the Crunch, Jaco and Legs. They were hoping that Wentworth would also join them, but he has not shown up yet. Since his mom died, he has been avoiding Big H and Crunch but Crunch has written her name, Susanna Wentworth on his T-shirt. Somewhere in the lineup is also Amelia, Carly, Sunny and Jennie. The Stegman kids make up the last group.

We are waiting for the sun to come up. The weather is cool this early. It is quiet, families huddle together, each group keeping a safe distance apart. Some are whispering, others are lost in thought. I recognise Pierre and Alain of the Sky House. Alain has been ill, he is still in a wheelchair, wearing an oxygen mask. He sees me looking and waves at me. Babi and Tannie Kotie are standing together, May and her husband have gone to visit their son. Max's brother and parents will only come back at the end of April. Ms Megan is standing next to Mom and Dad. She is taping the event for Uncle Luke and to share on the Starship Report. The Advocate has not come today, but he did call Adam to wish him well.

The sun finally peeks over the mountain. As it did a long time ago, it lights up Firefly's gleaming amber body shined to perfection by Dad. Liam checks the camera on my helmet again, then he gives a thumbs up. 'We are all set; my drone is up and ready.' Father Kingsley steps forward.

'Young people, are you ready for the task ahead?' We all nod, a few whispers, yes, we are all aware of the importance of the T-shirts we are wearing. He says a prayer, then he claps his hands together and sends us off. 'Go in faith!'

As always Adam takes the lead, followed by Khanyi, then Max. I bring up the rear. Our wheels sing on the tar road, we pick up speed, lean into the corners, pull lightly on the brakes. We flash past silent groups of people, a dog barking at a gate, doves scattering high. The tree roots are still there, we keep to the middle. An intersection is followed by the roundabout, then the final straight leading to St Michael's lies before us. We clear the slight kerb at the entrance and seconds later skid to a halt in front of the gleaming white St Michael's statue guarding the entrance to the cemetery. Adam struggles to get his helmet off, getting tangled in the oxygen mask. His brown eyes are sparkling and he lifts his hands for a double high five. Together we turn to watch the next batch of riders coming down St Michael's.

It took a pandemic, but Adam got his wish to fly down St. Michael's again.

www.ingramcontent.com/pod-product-compliance
Lightning Source LLC
LaVergne TN
LVHW091314150826
845673LV00006B/1641

* 9 7 8 1 0 6 7 2 3 7 7 4 5 *